Frank Clarke's
PAINTBOX 2

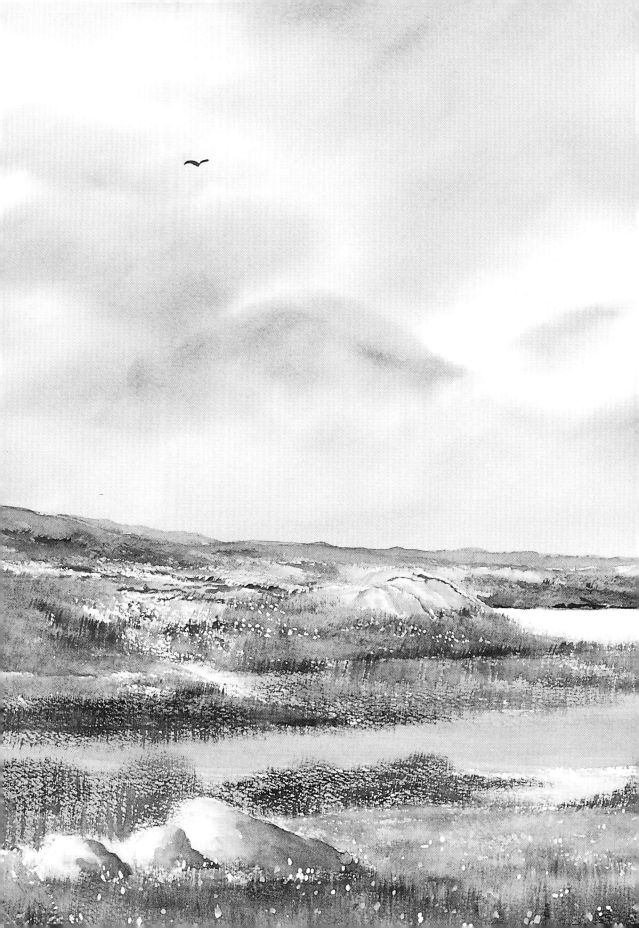

Frank Clarke's
PAINTBOX 2

Frank Clarke

To the many thousands of budding artists who purchased my first
BBC book, *Frank Clarke's Paintbox*, I thank you and hope *Paintbox 2*
will add to your enjoyment as well as whet the appetite of many
more new painters. This book is dedicated to you all.

Thanks to Nicola Copeland who was kind enough to offer me the opportunity of
writing a second BBC book and once again to my dedicated team – Isobel Gillan,
Charlotte Lochhead and Caroline Wainer – who banded together to help
produce and promote this book. To Peg, my wife, who provided the midnight
coffee. And to Catherine Cardiff who had the unenviable job of typing my scroll
(or should I say scrawl); those at Grange Golf Club, Dublin, and all at Craftnet and
Winsor & Newton for your help.

Published by BBC Worldwide Ltd,
Woodlands, 80 Wood Lane, London W12 0TT
First published in 2001
All text and artworks © Frank Clarke

All photographs by Ashley Morrison © BBC Worldwide Ltd, except those
on page 17 by Podge Kelly © BBC Worldwide Ltd and page 116 © Frank Clarke
Cover photograph by Ashley Morrison © BBC Worldwide Ltd, with artworks © Frank Clarke
The moral right of the author has been asserted

ISBN 0 563 53777 9

Commissioning editor: Nicola Copeland
Project editor: Charlotte Lochhead
Book designer and art director: Isobel Gillan

Set in Caslon, Futura and Gill Sans by BBC Worldwide Ltd
Printed and bound in France by Imprimerie Pollina S.A., N° L82686
Colour separations by Pace Colour Ltd, Southampton

Contents

My road to the brush

I am delighted to get another chance to write about my favourite subject, painting, and to share some more pictures with you. Those of you who know me, hello again, and those of you who are newcomers to painting, welcome! *Paintbox 2* has all the things a beginner needs to know to get started, and offers eight new step-by-step painting projects, lots of new drawing lessons and advice on things like painting outdoors or composing a painting from a photograph. I've also included a Gallery of extra paintings to give you even more pictures to work from and inspire you. There's something for everyone here, so I really hope you enjoy learning or continuing to paint.

Before we start painting I wanted to tell you something about 'my road to the brush'. I have travelled a lot since I wrote the first *Paintbox* book and some of the paintings we do here reflect the places I have visited. It seems life is full of all sorts of journeying, and I wanted to share with you my journey into the wonderful world of painting. It has been a joyful one and I hope you will enjoy making it, too.

I am not a trained artist and, being self-taught, I understand the problems you might find yourself experiencing when you start your painting journey. To be frank (excuse the pun), I had terrible trouble learning to paint. My greatest problem was when I told anyone I was trying to paint. They would usually say something like 'aren't you lucky to have the gift . . . I only wish I could draw a straight line'. It dawned on me that everyone was assuming that in order to paint I had to have some kind of gift or talent to begin with. My first efforts proved I didn't! What I did have, though, was a desire to paint and, luckily, a stubborn nature. When someone tells me I can't do something, I say 'why?'. Now I am not suggesting we can all run a four-minute mile just because we are determined, and neither am I suggesting that if we paint we'll all turn into Michelangelos. However, what I do know is that everyone can learn to paint if they want to, and that with some

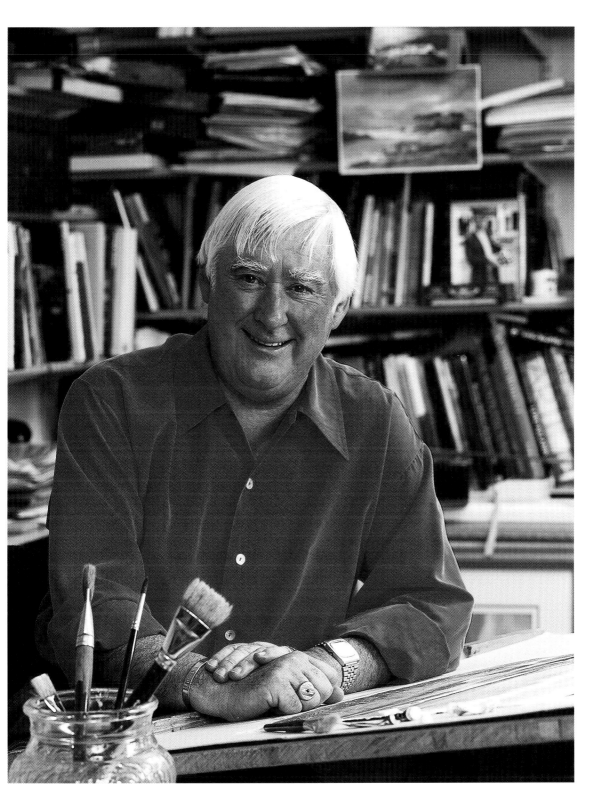

simple instructions to jump-start you – and that's what this book is all about – and some practise, you can become as good as you want.

Anyway, back to my journey into painting. Some years ago I had sold my business and, just for fun, I decided to try my hand at painting. I didn't know one end of a brush from the other and I thought that the word 'medium' (used so much in the art world to mean a multitude of different things) meant someone who spoke to the dead! My first port of call was one of Dublin's art shops to stock up on materials. The loud 'ding, dong' from the door bell and tall, not too well lit, shelves weren't ideal for settling the nerves of a budding artist. Neither was the elderly man, surrounded by piles of dog-eared advertising material, who seemed completely oblivious to my presence. Nevertheless, I began to select my equipment . . . and that's when my real problems began.

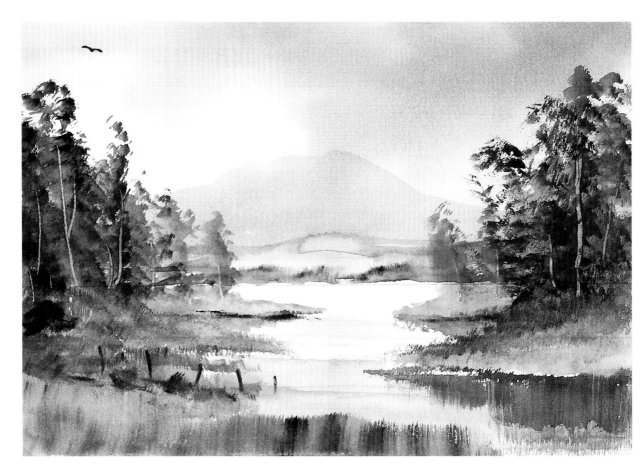

Which paint? There were racks of all the different types. I selected some oil colours. It made sense as there was a nice box of 12 tubes marked 'For beginners'. Then on to the brushes and, again, thousands confronted me. The only difference I could spot were that some were big and some small, and some were locked in a case and very expensive. I chose three brushes in large, medium and small because I liked the colours of their handles. I picked up a pad of paper and headed for the counter. I paid (not realizing that I had actually bought materials for oil, acrylic and watercolour painting) and made my way to a bookshop where I purchased a book on oil painting for beginners.

Reading my book I discovered my mistake, but I also discovered that the book's author had forgotten to write the most essential first few chapters of his book – the ones on how to get started. He, too, seemed to think that anyone painting a picture must have some sort of magic gift, so he didn't burden the artist with such trivial instructions as what brushes, colours and paint mixtures to use in order to paint the lovely cricket pitch scene on offer in the book.

Well, I'm pleased to say that things have changed since I started out and most art stores are now much more helpful and friendly. Books about painting, however, still seem to be missing the basic instructions. Just like learning to cook a recipe from a cookery book, painting a picture can be easy, but what you need is all the ingredients and all the instructions. One of the reasons for Delia Smith's success is that her recipes have clear, simple instructions – they start at the beginning and leave nothing out!

All the instructions for learning to paint are here, so why don't we get started on your journey and HAVE SOME MORE FUN!

Frank Clarke

Why should you paint?

The answer is easy – it's great fun! But there are many more reasons, so let's look at some of them.

Have you ever wondered why we give kids paints and colouring books, not only at home and school but also on planes and trains and in places like restaurants? The answer, we all know, is to keep them quiet. However, if children don't like doing something they won't do it, but it is rare to find a child who doesn't want to draw or paint. I think the reason for this is that painting fascinates, delights and interests them. It actually activates their brains and stimulates them to create something.

Let me tell you a story about three schools in America. They divided themselves in half and in one half of each school they included an art class on the curriculum. After a year they assessed the results. What they found was that the exam results of the children who had taken art classes were, on average, 20% better in every subject. So it seems that doing something creative can help in other aspects of learning and life, too.

Although it's not quite as straightforward as I'm making it here, in general, the right side of your brain is responsible for much of your creativity. Painting makes us exercise that side of our brains. The right side of your brain is also responsible for driving the left side of your body, so this could account for why many artists, writers, poets, etc. are left-handed. That's not to say that there aren't many who are right-handed also! When you use the creative part of your brain it is difficult to think of anything else and so it's easy to get away from all other worries or thoughts. That's why painting is considered such great therapy for people – it helps them forget and unwind.

It is a medical fact that an active brain helps towards keeping the body healthy. Henry Ford, the founder of the Ford Motor Company, once said, 'when you stop using your brain you die'. Did you ever

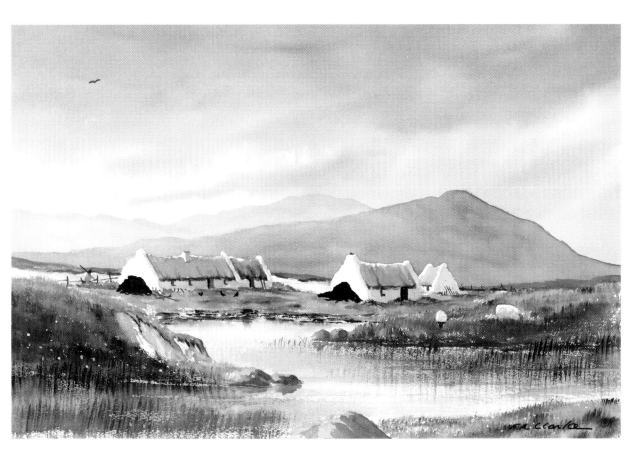

wonder why many artists live to a ripe old age? The answer may be that they have kept their brains active.

Apart from exercising your brain and improving your general learning ability, and apart from the fact that it's a great way to relax and forget your worries, painting also brings great satisfaction. Remember . . . painting comes from desire, it's not a gift, and if you have this desire then you can learn to paint and benefit from the huge amount of personal gratification you'll get from it. There is nothing more pleasing than displaying your first framed picture – not just to hear your friends and relations comment on how lovely your picture is or hear their disbelief that you painted it, but also for your own satisfaction at how well you have done and how much joy your picture and its sense of achievement brings you.

You can paint anywhere. I often do it on aircraft as it helps to pass the time. Boredom is probably one of the greatest causes of depression or of feeling useless and unfulfilled. Painting will soon put a stop to these feelings as it's impossible to be bored with a paintbrush!

What others say ...

I have often been accused that my Simply Painting technique for teaching people how to paint is *too* simple. However, I believe that the 'art' of teaching is to make to make it simple and fun, so as not to discourage people from making a start. I have selected extracts from some of the many thousands of letters I've received, to show you how easy learning to paint can be. I hope they will encourage you to learn and see the benefits painting can bring.

'About three months ago a group of us got together . . . to try our hand at painting . . . following your instructions very carefully. To say we have been delighted at the results would be a gross understatement. We are all amazed to find that what you say is true – anyone can paint! What has most surprised us is . . . we all wind up with completely different results.'

J. NEWMAN, WEST SUSSEX, ENGLAND

'I have just read and completed your new book, Frank Clarke's Paintbox, *and I would like to thank you. I really enjoyed learning with your no-nonsense, step-by-step teaching and the jargon-free wording.'*

S. WHITEWICK, NORTHUMBERLAND, ENGLAND

'For my 68th birthday, my wife bought me your book . . . I really enjoyed it immensely and had lots of fun. The exercises are quite brilliant and easy to follow. I've not painted since Junior School, some 60 years ago. Now retired . . . what I have missed!'

M. FOREMAN, WEST SUSSEX, ENGLAND

'I bought your book and I have been amazed at how easy it is to paint. I'm 66 years old and thanks to your book I've come alive again.'

B. HANSON, LANCASHIRE, ENGLAND

'My five-year-old is a dedicated Frank Clarke fan and the paints are taken out even before school in the mornings! We both attend an art class in the local community centre . . . thank you for giving the ordinary person like myself confidence to lift a brush.'

B. BRADY, CO DOWN, IRELAND

'After several attempts at art classes, I had convinced myself that I just wasn't artistic and would never understand the secrets of how to paint. Your book showed me there are no secrets, and I can't thank you enough for showing me that I am able to paint.'

C. MARSH, OXFORDSHIRE, ENGLAND

'I felt I had to write to say how much I appreciate your book, Paintbox. I am a newcomer to watercolour painting and thanks to inspiration from you I intend to make it more of a major hobby, because of the enjoyment I've already experienced.'

B. NOWELL, DURHAM, ENGLAND

'Thank you for producing such an inspirational and brilliant book . . . I read it from cover to cover and felt totally inspired and believed that I could paint. I have no doubt that without your encouragement and belief that anyone can do it, I would never have had a go and achieved a lifetime's wish. Thank you so very much.'

J. GARDNER, WARWICKSHIRE, ENGLAND

'I have just bought your Paintbox book and as a beginner I am finding it extremely helpful. It is a pleasure to be able to start from the beginning after many false starts with other publications.'

C. HADLEY, BIRMINGHAM, ENGLAND

Getting started

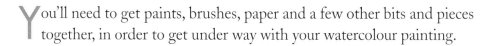

You'll need to get paints, brushes, paper and a few other bits and pieces together, in order to get under way with your watercolour painting.

PAINTS

I think watercolour paints are the best to learn with for several reasons:

- They are inexpensive to buy, and easy to use and transport
- They don't stain, don't smell and aren't toxic
- If you learn to paint with watercolours you will then be able to paint with any other medium, e.g. oils, acrylics, etc. The reverse is not the case . . . ask any oil painter!

Watercolours are packaged in two different ways: pans and tubes. Pans are small blocks of hardened paint pigment, like the stuff in those paint-boxes we all had as children. The paintbox usually had heaps of colours, and yet the only ones we ever seemed to use were the red, blue, yellow and green. Remember? You had to add lots of water and generally make quite a mess to get enough colour to paint on your paper.

Tubes come ready to use and are easier to mix, in my opinion. They are also much easier to store. Just put the tops on and they are ready for your next painting session. I recommend you use tubes. Student quality Cotman paint, made by Winsor & Newton, is good stuff – if you are feeling extravagant you can purchase artist's quality paint, but I find the student quality works just fine. You don't need a huge selection of colours. With those shown here and captioned below you can mix any other colour you need, so start with these eight colours:

PAINTS *top to bottom* Ultramarine blue, Lemon yellow, Alizarin crimson, Cobalt blue, Payne's grey, Light red, Raw sienna and Burnt umber; *opposite top* Permanent white designers' gouache.

It may be tempting to buy the very cheap boxes of watercolour tubes, but even though the colours have the same names you may that they are mixed in a different way and can be inconsistent. Th: might make it hard to match the colours needed for the paintings this book, so it is worth sticking with the better-known brands ev though they might seem more expensive. Watercolour tubes last f(ages as you only use a little paint at a time, so the investment is worthwhile and you won't be sorry.

There's one more tube of paint you'll need. It's an opaque paint called designers' gouache and you should get a tube of permanent white. It is a great help when painting the crests of waves on the s highlights on fruit and flowers, etc.

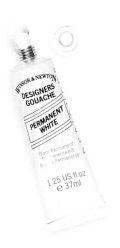

BRUSHES AND HOW TO USE THEM

There are three main brushes in my paintbox. Two are made from goathair and one from nylon.

My large goathair is a flat 1½-inch (38-mm) brush and my small one is a flat ¾-inch (19-mm) brush. I call them my obedient brushes because whichever way you bend the hair on them (see right and below) it doesn't spring back as it would on nylon, sable or bristle brushes. They really are best if made of goathair because they're easier to use, but any watercolour brushes of the same dimensions are better than not painting at all!

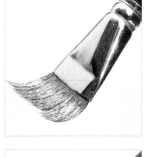

BRUSHES My obedient small and large goathair brushes and my rigger.

One of the main reasons for using a large brush as your workhorse is that it allows you to cover large areas quickly, which I feel is vital when painting landscapes in watercolour. We usually want to use small brushes when we start out, thinking that we can't do much damage with a little brush. Don't be afraid to use your big brush! It makes painting a lot easier (as you will discover) and it will soon become your best friend.

My nylon brush is called a no.3 rigger (or liner) and because it springs back into shape I can use it like a pen or pencil. I use it to do fine line work or fill in smaller areas of the page.

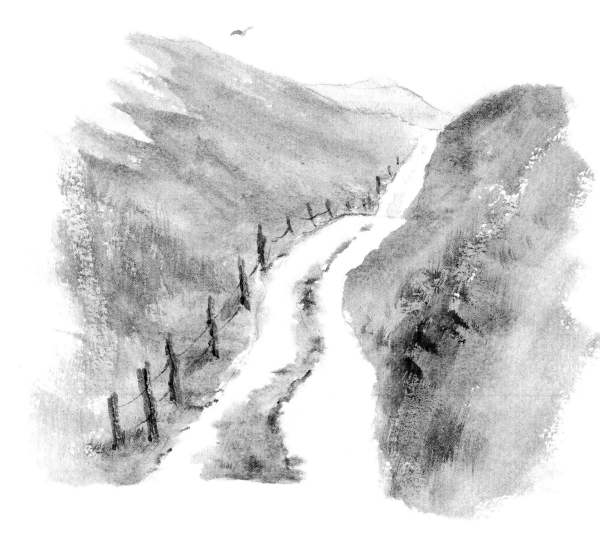

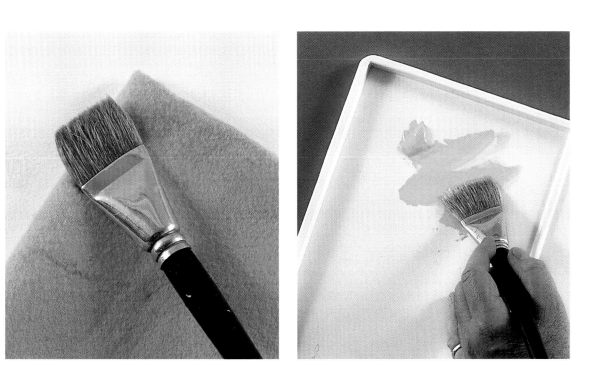

Holding your brush

I'm left-handed so don't get confused! Hold your brushes firmly, like
you would a pen, and practise (see pages 18–19) to get used to them.

Controlling the water

When using your large and small goathair brushes you'll need to control
the water on them by getting rid of the excess on a cloth. Every time you
dip a flat brush in water you should rest the body of the brush on your
folded cloth. Keep the tip away from the cloth to keep it moist, but soak
up the bulk of the water from the body of the brush bristles. You should
do this each time you clean your brush, except when painting skies
when you'll need to have a fairly wet brush before you mix your paint.

Mixing the paint

To mix paint with water you need only a small blob of colour on your
palette. Keep your brush (which will be moistened but rid of the excess
water) flat and, using its corner, lift some paint into the centre of the
palette. Move the brush gently from left to right to load the paint, then
turn it over and load the other side of the bristles in the same way.

Brush strokes

Before you get painting the step-by-step pictures, it's a good idea to try out your brushes and practise some of the brush strokes you'll need to give you confidence. Because our brushes are so obedient, they allow us to do several different types of brush strokes:

Hold the large brush, with the bristles horizontal and lying almost flat against the paper, and sweep across horizontally to cover large areas like skies.

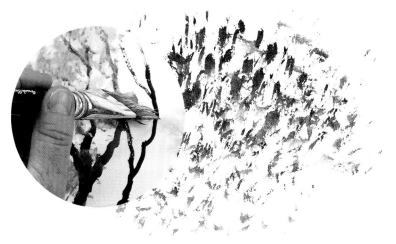

An almost dry large brush, loaded with a tiny bit of paint, can create a stippled effect if you hold the brush vertically over your paper, with bristle tips pointing directly down, and lightly dab onto the paper. This stippling is used to form leaves on your trees or bushes in the foreground.

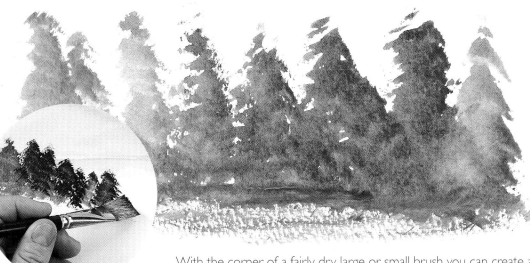

With the corner of a fairly dry large or small brush you can create a pointed shape. Dab the brush corner up the page, from the base to the tip of the tree, to form evergreens and conifers.

Paint trees from the bottom up. Use the rigger tip, pressing it more at the base for a thicker line. Lift as you go up and the line gets thinner. Drag branches out from the trunk, lifting and flicking as you go. Dragging and lifting also creates wispy grass blades.

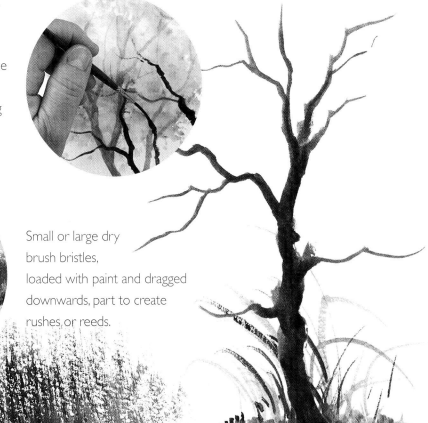

Small or large dry brush bristles, loaded with paint and dragged downwards, part to create rushes or reeds.

PAPER

I am often asked, 'Why do I have to use watercolour paper?' The answer is because it's made in a special way to stop your paint soaking into the surface, and it doesn't buckle or disintegrate when constantly made wet or rubbed with brush bristles. However, there are many different types of watercolour paper – they come in different surfaces, thicknesses and sizes – and all this will seem very complicated to the beginner, so let's see if I can demystify what it all means.

Watercolour paper is made from wood pulp, glue and cotton (sometimes called 'rag'). At least half the content of your paper should be cotton, and it needs to be well glued so it doesn't disintegrate when you're painting. If you stick to the well-known manufacturers of quality paper, you won't come unstuck! Winsor & Newton's Cotman range of paper is very reliable, and other good brands are Archer's, Daler-Rowney, Fabrians and Whatman.

Watercolour paper is different to other types of paper because during its manufacture the paper is pressed and immersed in a bath of thin gelatinous mixture, made from glue, clay or even wax. This process is called 'sizing' and it seals the surface of the paper, making your paint stay on the surface rather than soak in. Watercolour paper comes in three different surfaces:

- **Cold Pressed** which has a slight grain on the surface. It is the most commonly used, and I recommend you start painting using this type of watercolour paper. For some bizarre reason it is sometimes described as 'medium' and sometimes as 'cold pressed'. I don't know why they can't make up their minds!
- **Hot Pressed** which has a very smooth surface.
- **Rough** which has, as you might have guessed, a rough surface. Because it has an uneven surface it makes the brush jump over the bumps and produces unusual effects. I would advise you to stay away from rough paper until you have painted for a while.

All these papers come in different thicknesses and the thicker a piece of paper is, the more it weighs and the more expensive it is. Paper is sold according to its weight. (Confusingly, the weighing is done using an old printer's measure of 500 sheets to get the imperial pound weight but only a single sheet per square metre for the metric gram weight – that's why there are two different weights on the front of any pad of paper you see.) What thickness you use depends on things like how aggressively you apply your paint, how many times you go over and over the paper surface and how large you want your picture to be. Luckily you don't have to worry about all this as I can advise you, but generally the trick is to purchase the lightest paper that will produce the best results for the size of painting you want to paint.

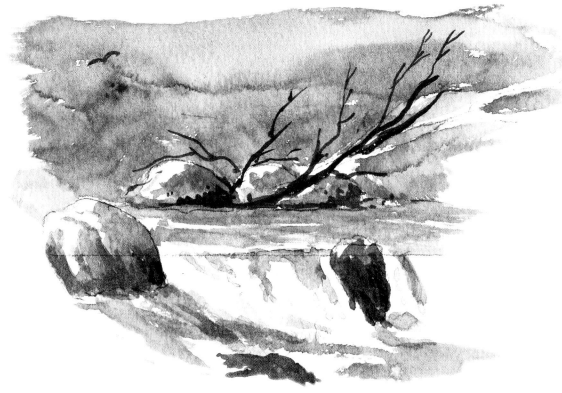

Paper weights start at about 80lb/170gsm and go up to about 400lb/850gsm. I recommend 140lb/300gsm. The reason is that all the pictures we paint in this book are 10 × 14 inches (255 × 355 mm) in size and if I used a lighter paper it would cockle (buckle) with the amount of paint, water and layers we put on. If we were painting larger watercolours we would use the thicker, more sturdy, paper.

My general estimates are for a picture size of:
- Up to 12 × 16 inches (305 × 406 mm) use 140lb/300gsm paper
- Up to 15 × 22 inches (375 × 558 mm) use 250lb/535gsm paper
- Over 15 × 22 inches (375 × 558 mm) use at least 300lb/640gsm paper

You can buy your paper in different ways: glued or wired pads, or single sheets that can be cut to whatever size you want. This is tricky so I advise using a pad of white, cold pressed, watercolour paper, weighing 140lb/300gsm and measuring 10 × 14 inches (255 × 355 mm). Either wired or glued will do, but get a pad as it's easier to deal with and carry about!

TAKING CARE OF YOUR EQUIPMENT

It's really important to look after your watercolour materials and equipment and to clean and store them properly so that they last.

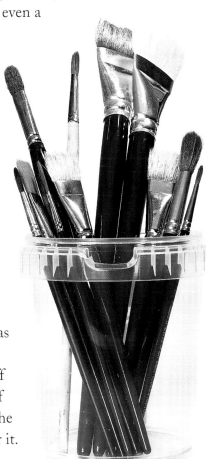

- **Paints** should always have the tube tops replaced as soon as you've squeezed out what you need. Always keep the tops clean otherwise they become difficult to open, particularly if you don't paint very often. If the tube tops do stick, pinch a clothes peg (or even a small nutcracker) onto the top to give you extra grip and leverage.

- **Brushes** are very easy to clean: just wash them in some slightly soapy water and rinse really well with lots of clean water. Lay them flat to dry or stand them, with bristles pointing up, in a pot. The bristles should not be bent, pushed or folded over, and never put the brushes back in your paintbox with the bristles pushed against the end of the box. Always make sure the box is large enough to allow the brush to lay flat.

- **Paper** should be handled with care. When I started to paint I found little round spots appeared when I laid a wash (put a coat of paint on the paper). I thought it was a fault in the paper and wrote to the manufacturers. They were kind enough to explain 'keep your hands off the paper'. The tips of your fingers can be greasy and if you touch the paper too much the grease transfers to the paper, thus causing circular marks when you paint over it. So, hands off!

OTHER THINGS YOU'LL NEED

As well as your brushes, paints and paper, you'll also need to collect up some other items before we can get started on a picture.

- A white plate or small white tray to act as a palette (to mix your paint on)
- A large pot to hold your water
- Some absorbent old cloths to wipe your brushes on
- An ordinary pencil (HB is fine but 2B erases better when you're sketching a lot)
- A ruler
- An eraser
- A flat board measuring approximately 16 × 20 inches (410 × 508 mm) to stick your paper on. It's easier to paint on a sloping surface so find a large book about $2\frac{1}{2}$ inches (6.5 cm) thick to prop your board against

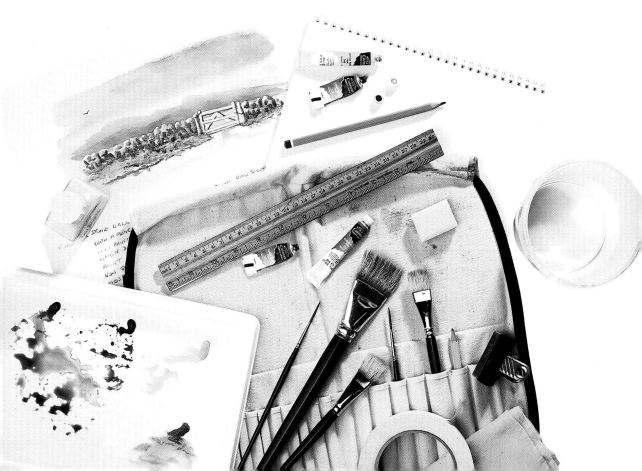

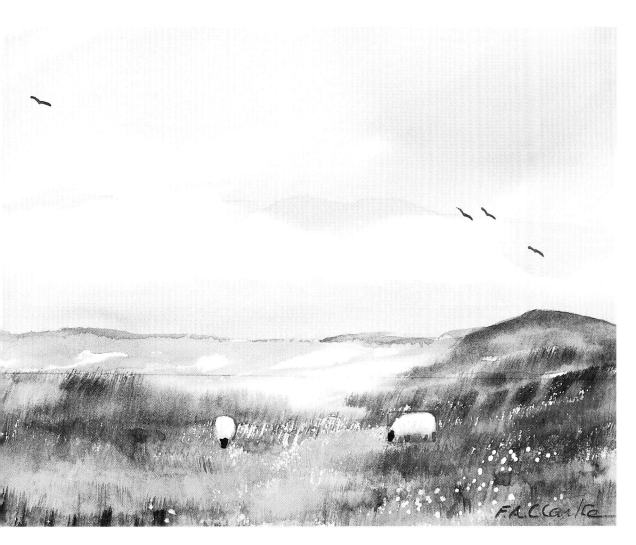

- Masking tape to stick the paper onto the board
- Masking fluid (available at your art shop, see page 29 for advice on how to use it)
- An old, small brush if you have one (for applying masking fluid, or you can use your rigger)
- Hair dryer

Handy tip: It's really useful to have a hair dryer to help dry parts of your painting. If you don't have one, though, a little patience and perhaps the odd coffee break is all that's needed!

How the Simply Painting system works

To do any hobby you need two things: a desire to partake of it and a knowledge of the basic fundamentals. Without these, I believe, it is impossible to enjoy your endeavours. The first is simple – you must have it already if you're reading this! The second requires help and that's where I come in. What I wouldn't have given for some basic help when I started! Sadly, the books and art classes I experienced assumed I already knew the basics. I won't make the same mistake with you! If you know the next part, you can skip a few pages while the beginners catch up.

The hardest part of painting a picture is plucking up the courage to start and knowing *where* to start. To make the process easier, I devised a foolproof system – my Simply Painting system – to get you started. It's called 'Have Some More Fun', and fun it *is*! I promise, if you follow this system you *will* be able to paint wonderful pictures and you'll find the more you paint the better you become. I've never met anyone who couldn't paint and once you realize you can do it too, you'll improve rapidly. You *can* paint, so don't let anyone tell you otherwise!

Now, let's Have Some More Fun. The first letter of each word has a significance and is designed to help you remember the order in which to paint various areas of your landscape and remind you to have fun!

HORIZON **H** have

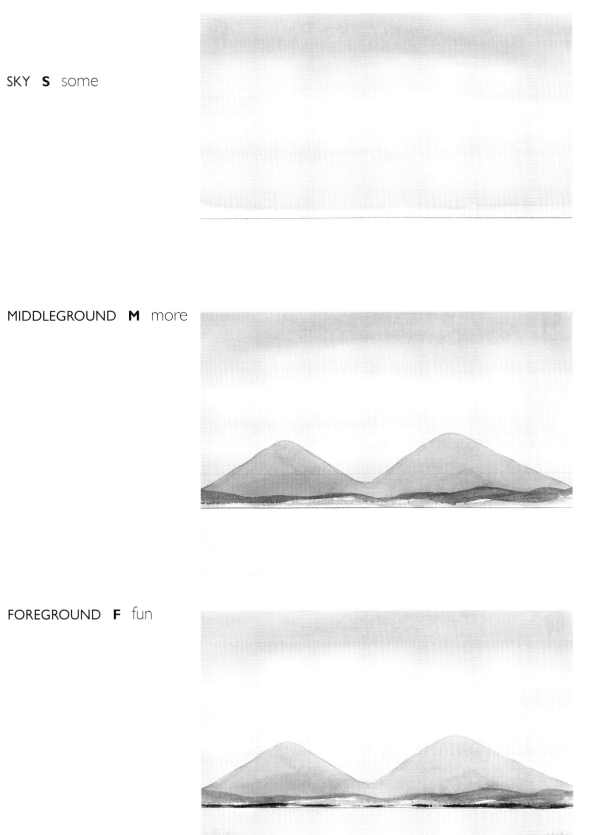

SKY **S** some

MIDDLEGROUND **M** more

FOREGROUND **F** fun

Things to remember when you paint

For all the painting projects in this book, here are a few reminders of things you'll need to bear in mind when painting the pictures:

- **Read the painting project through** and really study the finished painting before you start. Remember to keep looking carefully at the steps as you go, so you know what you are trying to add to your picture.
- **Each lesson uses** a piece of white, 10 × 14-inch (255 × 355-mm), 140lb/300gsm watercolour paper. Use the paper landscape (or lengthways) and portrait (or upright), as instructed.
- **Prop up your board** by about 2½ inches (6.5 cm). Find a large book to lean your board on so that it slopes and the top edge of the paper is higher than the bottom. It's easier to paint on a sloping surface and it helps control the paint when you're doing large areas like skies.
- **When I say** '*large brush*' I mean your 1½-inch (38-mm) goathair and '*small brush*' means your ¾-inch (19-mm) goathair. A '*dry brush*' means one well dried on your cloth but not completely bone dry. '*Dry it*' refers to drying your painting with a hairdryer, if you have one, or let it dry naturally if you don't. '*Stipple*' means downward dabs of a large or small brush, making sure it's been dried well on your cloth before loading your paint, otherwise the bristles won't separate (see page 18).
- **Use a large water pot** – a big, plastic, fizzy drink bottle, cut in half, is ideal. You won't need to change your water if the pot is large enough.
- **Clean your brushes** between paint mixes – I won't be reminding you to do this all the time: it should become habit!
- **Control the water on your large and small goathair brushes** every time you clean them. Get into the habit of always using your cloth to soak up the excess water each time (see page 17 for a reminder, if you need it).
- **Test your colour** on a scrap of paper. Adding more water will make it paler or adding more paint from the tube will make it darker, or you may need to adjust the balance of the two colours you've mixed.

- **Using masking fluid** is easy. It is a liquid rubber latex which you paint on your paper to protect areas you want to keep white. If you buy the slightly yellow variety you can see it more easily once it's on your paper. If you have a spare old, small brush to use with the fluid it helps, but if not, use your rigger. It dries quite fast and can clog your brush, so dip your brush in water before you dip it in the masking fluid and paint for no more than 20 seconds before dipping back into the water again and reloading with more masking fluid.

  Be certain the fluid on your paper is dry before painting over it. Once your paint is dry, use a clean finger or an eraser to rub the masking fluid off. Rub towards the centre of the masked area and away from the painted edge so, if the paper tears, it will not rip your painted surface.

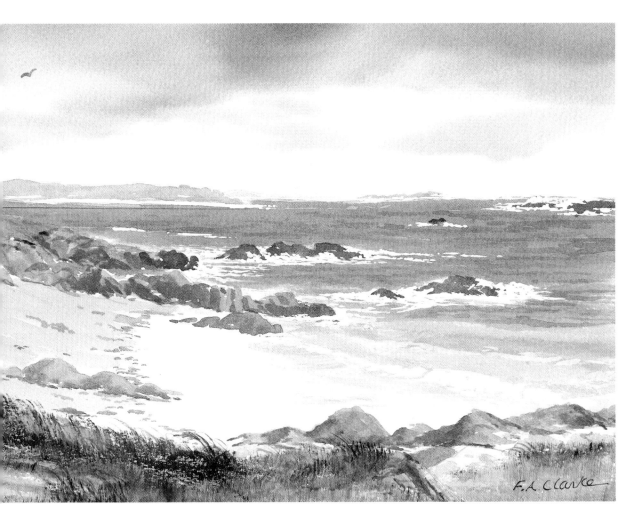

Let's paint a picture!

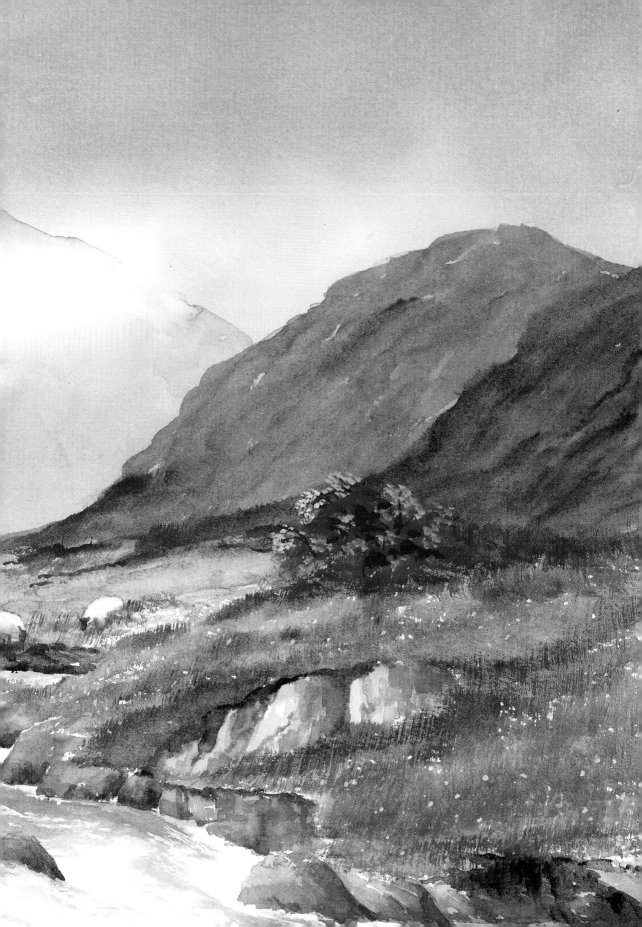

mountains and lake

Let's begin with a simple scene which illustrates my Have Some More Fun technique. It shows how to divide a painting into Horizon, Sky, Middle and Foreground areas and will give you confidence in your ability to paint. Remember to control the water on your brush (see page 17) and dry your painting – naturally or using your hairdryer – when it says 'dry this'.

you will need

- Paint: Raw sienna, Cobalt blue, Lemon yellow and Burnt umber
- Brushes: your large (1½-inch) brush and no.3 rigger
- Paper: a sheet of 10 × 14-inch (255 × 355-mm) 140lb/300gsm watercolour paper
- Palette (your white plate or tray)
- Water pot

- Cloths
- Pencil and ruler
- Eraser
- Board: 16 × 20 inches (410 × 508 mm) to stick your paper on
- Masking tape to stick the paper onto the board
- Hairdryer, if you have one

1

1 HORIZON Using masking tape across the corners, fix your sheet of paper lengthways onto your board. With a pencil, draw the horizon line about 2½ inches (6.5 cm) up from the paper's bottom edge. Mine's quite dark so you can see it, but yours can be lighter. Prop up the board. You need speed when painting skies as the first paint layer needs to be damp when you put on the second … but don't panic!

2 SKY Put some Raw sienna and Cobalt blue on your palette. Using your large brush, mix some Raw sienna with water. Hold the brush flat against the paper and paint in broad strokes right across, going from the top, down to within half an inch of the horizon line.

3 While this is wet, clean the brush and mix the Cobalt blue with water. Paint in sweeps of blue, down to within half an inch of the horizon line, leaving some patches of Raw sienna showing through. Be confident, paint quickly and don't fiddle! Dry this.

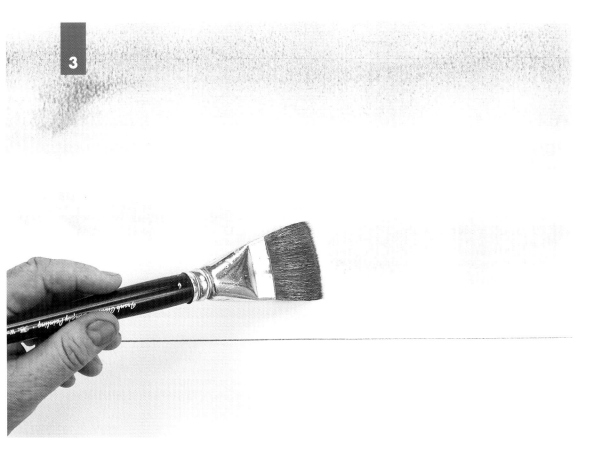

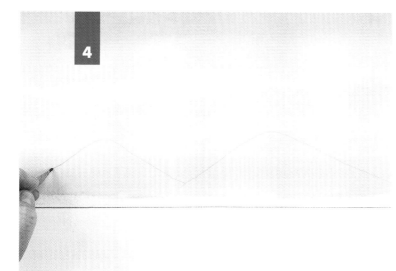

4 MIDDLEGROUND With a pencil lightly draw the letter 'm' on the horizon line. This forms your mountains. You can paint them straight in (see step 5), but if this is your first picture I suggest you draw them first.

5 Using your large brush, mix a little Raw sienna into your Cobalt blue paint. Be careful – don't add too much: about 5% Raw sienna will do. Paint in the mountains. Do this quickly, in big strokes and, again, don't fiddle. Dry this. Clean your brush.

6 Mix Lemon yellow with a little Raw sienna. Hold your brush tip horizontal, and paint vegetation across the base of the mountains. You can go over it a little, but stay above the horizon. While this is wet, add more Raw sienna so the mix is now 50% of each and paint across again, covering some patches of the vegetation.

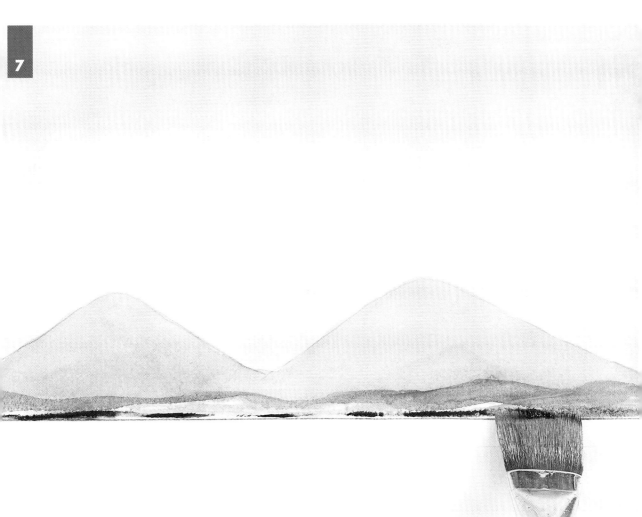

7 Again, while this is still wet, dab some neat Burnt umber across the base of this. Go along the horizon line and leave some places untouched to give a realistic impression of a riverbank. Dry this.

8 FOREGROUND Still using your large brush and with the same mix that you used for the mountains (5% Raw sienna and 95% Cobalt blue), sweep the paint across the paper below the riverbank. Continue down to the bottom of the page. You may have to go across the paper several times, that's fine, but don't stop a brush stroke half way. Go all the way across, otherwise you'll get marks where you don't want them. Dry this.

Handy tip: In most cases water in the middleground or foreground of a picture reflects the colours used in the sky.

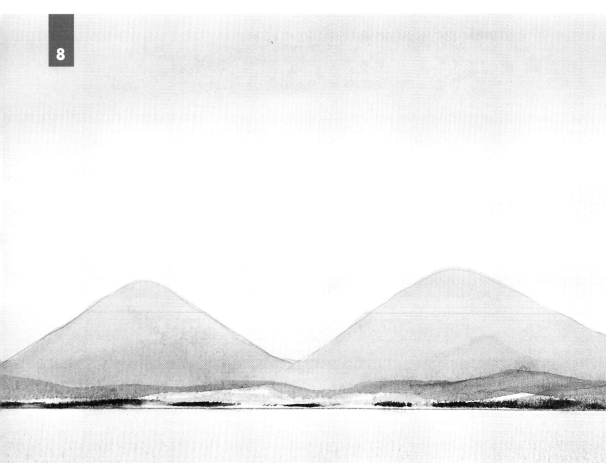

8

9 For the reeds and rushes, make sure your large brush is almost dry and use plenty of paint. Load some neat Raw sienna onto the large brush. Start at one side of the paper and paint in some rushes using light downward strokes (see page 19 if you need a reminder).

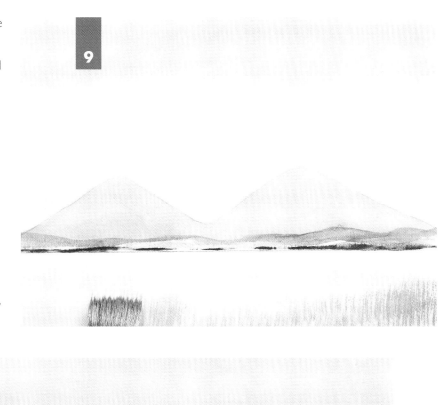

10 Without cleaning your brush, load some neat Burnt umber onto it. Paint some reeds using the same light downward strokes, covering only parts of the rushes.

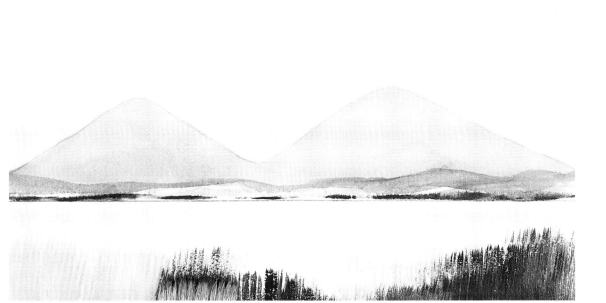

MOUNTAINS AND LAKE

Well done. You only have to add my friend, Joe the bird, and you've completed your painting. He's just a small, flattened 'v' made with some Burnt umber on your rigger brush. Practise on a scrap of paper first if you want. You can even add him with a fine black pen if you'd rather. Now sign your painting and frame it – you'll be amazed how much this enhances it.

Handy tip: To paint a graduated, even, unstreaky sky you only have about two minutes before the paint starts drying. Often the sky gets lighter nearer the horizon so mix in more water as you paint down the page. Always mix up enough paint before you begin and use lots of water so that one brush stroke of paint merges with the next, avoiding hard lines and streaks. Be bold and don't hang about!

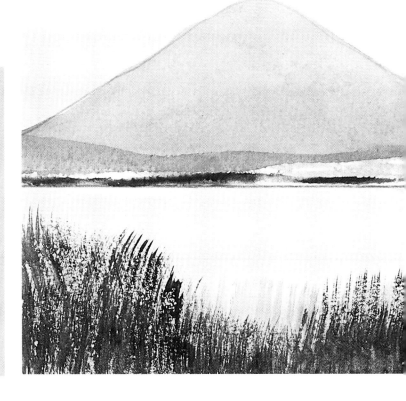

misty pond

My pond has a single-colour, flat wash sky, which means it's one colour – a purple mist – from top to bottom. This makes it an easy sky to paint! Take your time mixing the colours for this picture and test them on a scrap of paper first to check they are what you want.

you will need

- Paint: Cobalt blue, Alizarin crimson, Burnt umber, Raw sienna and Lemon yellow
- Brushes: your large (1½-inch) brush, small (¾-inch) brush and no.3 rigger
- Paper: a sheet of 10 × 14-inch (255 × 355-mm) 140lb/300gsm watercolour paper
- Palette (your white plate or tray)
- Water pot
- Cloths
- Pencil and ruler
- Eraser
- Board: 16 × 20 inches (410 × 508 mm) to stick your paper on
- Masking tape to stick the paper onto the board
- Hairdryer, if you have one

1

1 HORIZON Using masking tape across the corners, fix your sheet of paper lengthways onto your board. With a pencil, draw the horizon line about 3½ inches (9 cm) up from the paper's bottom edge. Prop up the board.

2 SKY With your large brush, mix Cobalt blue and Alizarin crimson. Clean the brush. Using only clean water on your large brush, wet the paper down to within half an inch of the horizon line. Quickly, while this is damp, paint in the sky with the brush flat and using broad, sweeping horizontal strokes.

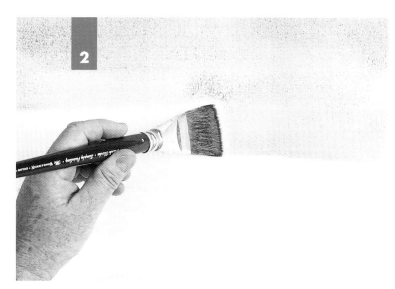

3 MIDDLEGROUND Again, while the paper is wet, mix more Cobalt blue and Alizarin crimson with a tiny bit of Burnt umber to darken it. Use the corner of the large brush, lightly dabbing up the length of each tree. Level them off at the base but stay above the horizon. Dab over again if you need to darken them slightly, but do this while the paper is damp so you don't get hard edges, just a lovely, soft, misty effect of trees.

4 Add distant trunks, while the trees are still wet, by scraping a few lines into the paint with your fingernail.

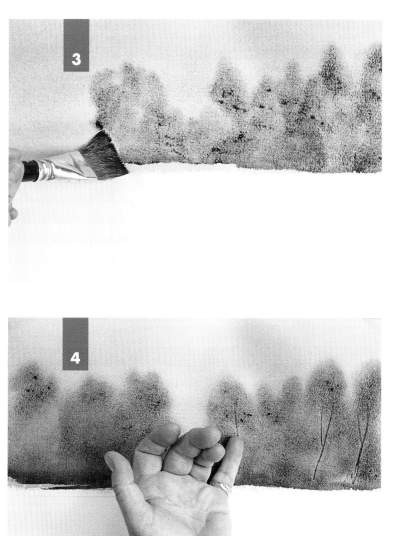

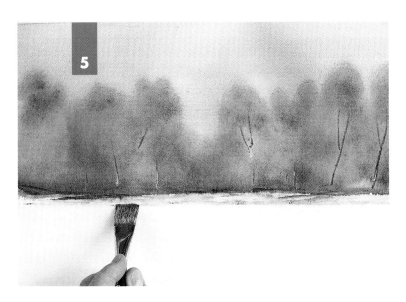

5 For the riverbank bushes, above the horizon line, use your small brush. Load on some Raw sienna and dab the bristle tips horizontally across the riverbank. Where you overlap the trees the paint will darken slightly. Using your tree mix of Cobalt blue, Alizarin crimson and Burnt umber, dab across the base of the bushes to form a mottled riverbank edge to meet the horizon line.

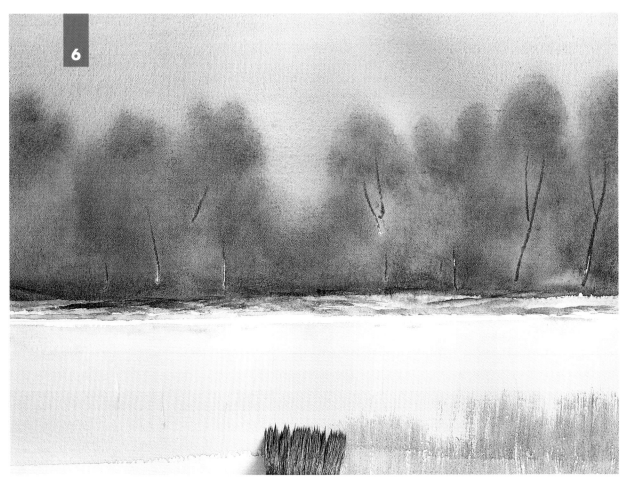

6 FOREGROUND The pond is a slightly more watery version of the sky: Cobalt blue and Alizarin crimson. Leave a tiny gap of white below the horizon line and start below this, working down the paper. Use your large brush flat, in sweeping strokes. Stop before the bottom of the paper. While damp, use Raw sienna on a clean, dry large brush and dab in some patches below the riverbank. Scrape the tree reflections into the water. Dry this. On a dry large brush, take more Raw sienna and dab in downward strokes of grass.

7 With Burnt umber on a dry large brush, do the same to create some reeds and rushes over the grass. Use your rigger and Burnt umber and paint in the main trunk of your tree, working from the base up. Add the branches (see page 19 for a reminder). Dry this.

Handy tip: Before you add a tree to your painting, practise one on a piece of scrap paper first to give you confidence.

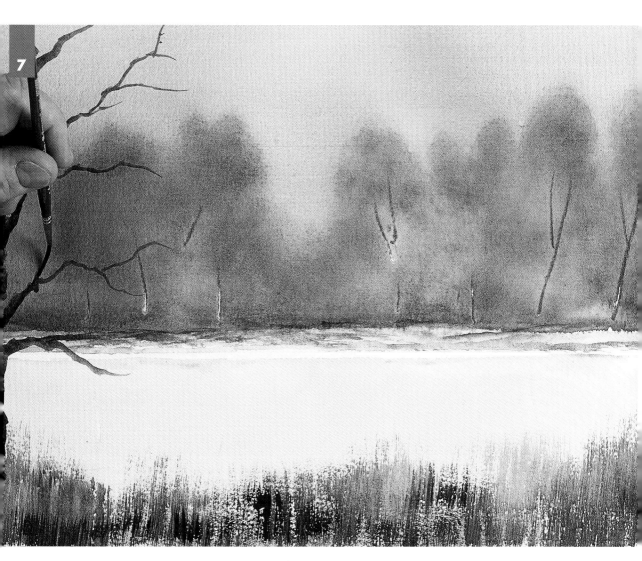

8 For the leaves of the tree, clean your large brush and mix Lemon yellow and a tiny bit of Cobalt blue to get a light green. Dry your brush, then use its corner to stipple in some light green leaves along the branches of the tree. Work from the branch tips back towards the trunk. Don't be afraid to attack the paper, but don't overwork it and add too much paint either! Dry this.

9 Add a bit more Cobalt blue to the leaf mix to darken it. With a dry large brush, stipple in some darker leaves, keeping patches of light showing through. Clean and dry your brush. Load some Raw sienna mixed with a little Lemon yellow and Burnt umber and stipple in a bush at the tree base. Dry this. Darken the paint with more Burnt umber and add a second layer. Use Burnt umber on your rigger to paint another tree.

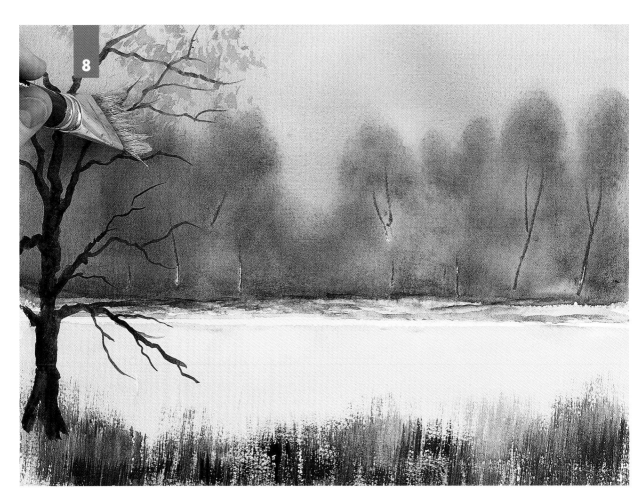

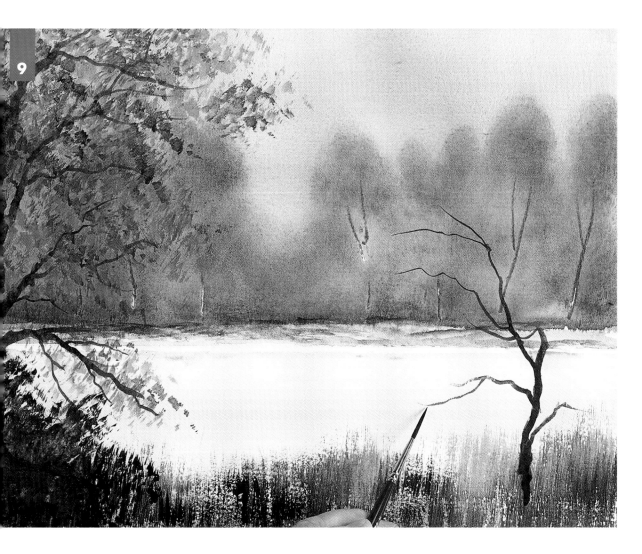

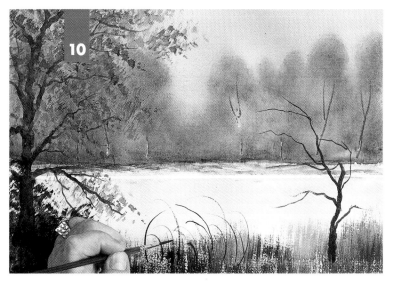

9

10 Still using your rigger and Burnt umber, paint in some wispy reeds and rushes. Start at their bases and drag the brush up, lifting it – almost flicking it – in a curve and off the paper as you go. Continue across to the right adding wisps under your second tree, too. Dry this.

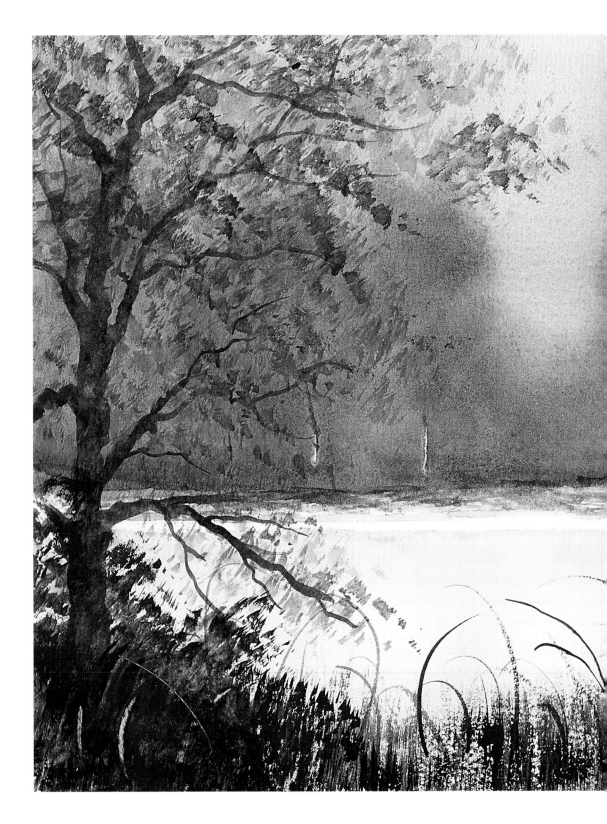

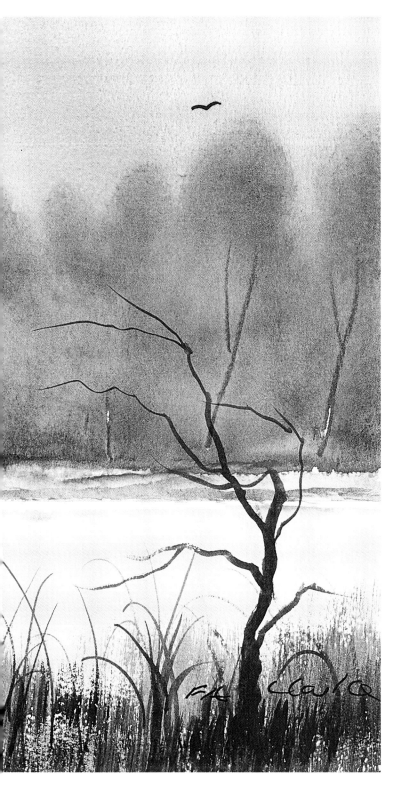

MISTY POND

'Ground' your second tree by adding some dark grass beneath it. Use a dry large brush and some Burnt umber and add a few downward strokes at the tree's base. With the same paint on your rigger add Joe the bird and there you go, a beautiful misty pond ready to sign and frame.

Handy tip: Don't be afraid of your rigger. Hold it like you would a pen – it's just like an old-fashioned quill. Its tip will produce a very fine line for painting things like Joe the bird but, if you want, you can always use a dark pen instead to paint him in.

rolling **river**

The Rio Grande is a huge river that winds its way through rugged mountains in New Mexico. The area I visited wasn't very green and, with the dry desert landscape, scrub bushes and distant purple mountains, the colours were rich and earthy.

you will need

- Paint: Cobalt blue, Light red, Lemon yellow, Raw sienna and Burnt umber
- Brushes: your large (1½-inch) brush, small (¾-inch) brush and no.3 rigger
- Paper: a sheet of 10 × 14-inch (255 × 355-mm) 140lb/300gsm watercolour paper
- Palette (your white plate or tray)
- Water pot
- Cloths
- Pencil and ruler
- Eraser
- Board: 16 × 20 inches (410 × 508 mm) to stick your paper on
- Masking tape to stick the paper onto the board
- Hairdryer, if you have one

1

1 HORIZON Using masking tape across the corners, fix your sheet of paper lengthways onto your board. With a pencil, draw the horizon line about 4½ inches (11.5 cm) up from the paper's bottom edge. Prop up the board.

2 SKY With your large brush, mix Cobalt blue with some water and paint in broad sweeps horizontally, down to just above the horizon line. Leave some white spaces to represent the clouds in patches. Dry this.

3 MIDDLEGROUND For the mountains, with your small brush mix 50% Cobalt blue and 50% Light red. Paint in your jagged outline and fill in the area down to just above the horizon line. Quickly move to step 4!

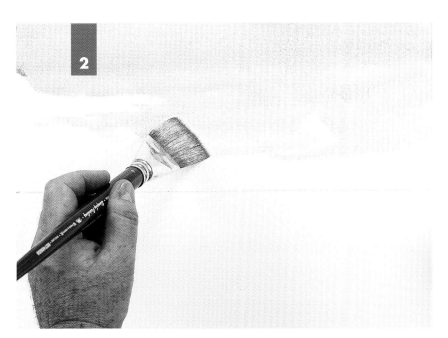

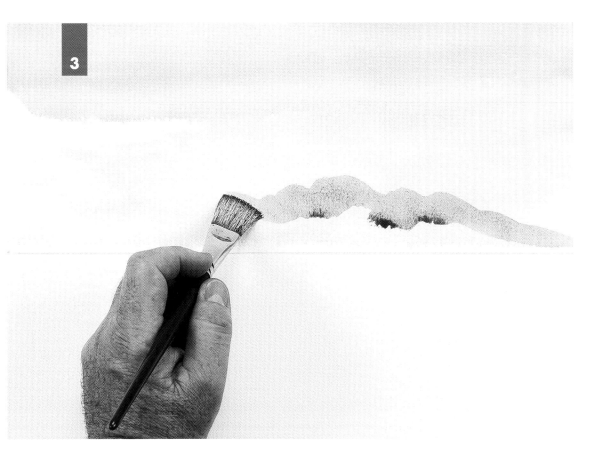

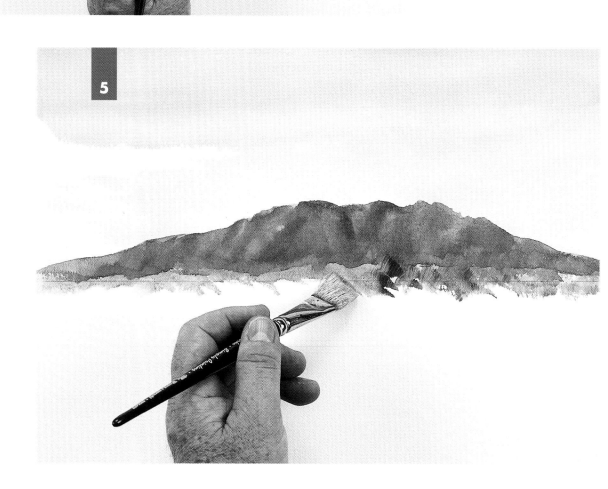

4 Work while the paint is still damp and add more Light red to the mix to fill in some darker patches on the top of the mountains. Dab these on in downward slanting strokes from top to bottom to create gullies, craggy rocks and shaded parts on the surface of the mountains. Go over patches again if you need to darken even further. Dry this.

5 For the bushes on the far riverbank, spreading to just below the horizon line, use your small brush and mix 75% Lemon yellow with 25% Light red. Use the corner of the brush and dab across leaving a few little patches of white.

6 For the flat land between the bushes and the river's edge, mix Lemon yellow with a tiny bit of Cobalt blue to create a greeny yellow colour. Sweep this across with your small brush. Mix some Raw sienna and a tiny bit of Burnt umber and use your brush like a chisel to dab some broken dark areas of bush either side of the flat land.

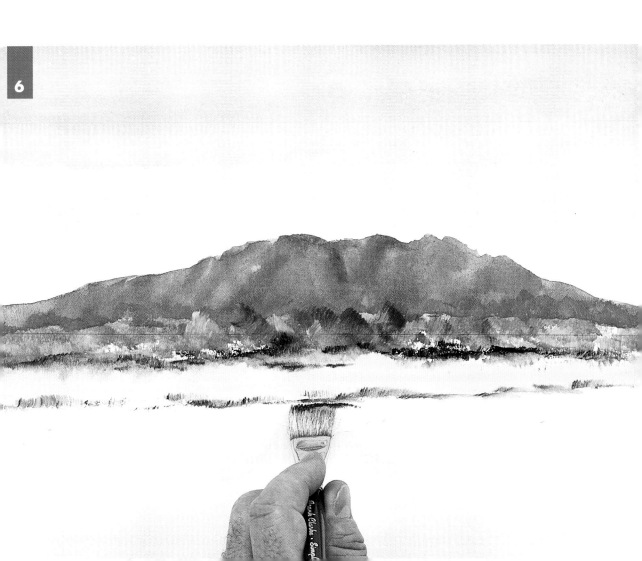

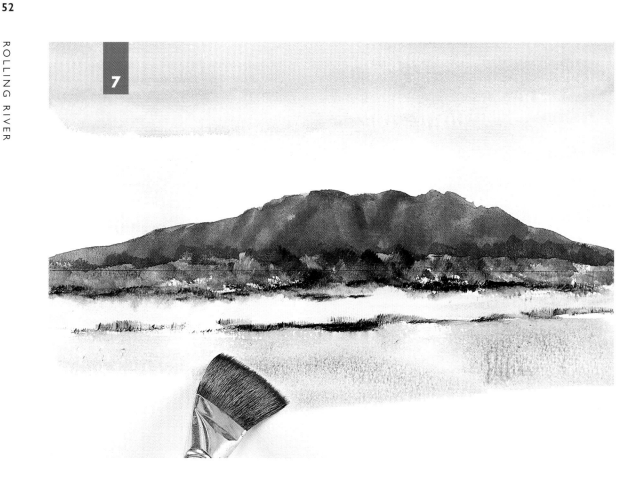

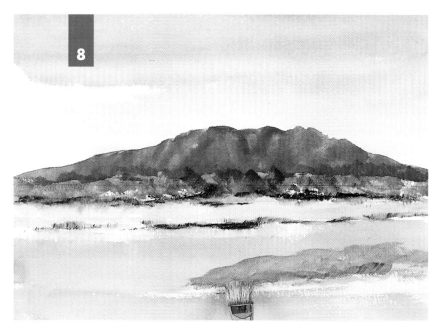

7 FOREGROUND For the river, use your large brush and watery Cobalt blue and sweep across in broad strokes to the bottom of your paper. Go over this again but leave a patch untouched on the right side where the little piece of land sticking out will go (you'll see in the next step!). Dry this.

8 For this jutting land, use your small brush, fairly dry with a mixture of Raw sienna, Lemon yellow and a tiny bit of Light red. Dry this.

9 Mix Lemon yellow with a little Cobalt blue to make green. Use the corner of a fairly dry small brush and dab in the trees from their bases on the land, up. While still wet …

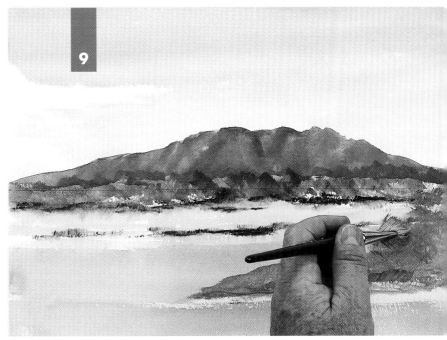

10 Quickly, scratch in a few tree trunks with a fingernail. Still using your green, add a patch of grass away to the left of the tree bases. Dry this.

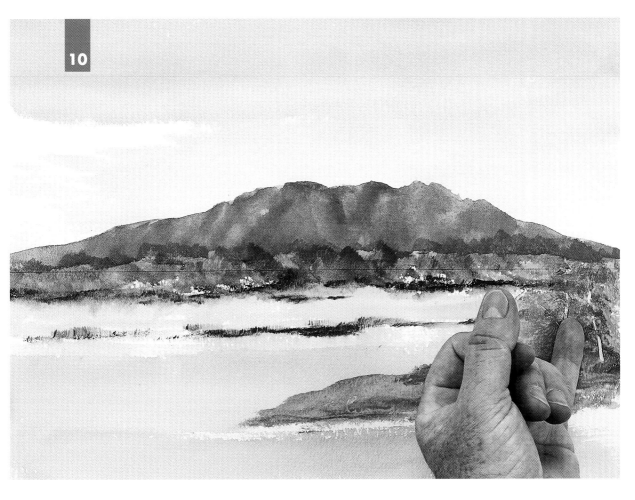

11 Mix Burnt umber with a little Light red and add some tree shadows coming across from the bases of the tree trunks. Dab along the edge of the riverbank, too, to create some darker areas in the water.

12 For the grass on the near riverbank, use a large brush and mix Lemon yellow with a tiny bit of Cobalt blue and Raw sienna. Use the brush tip horizontally and make downward strokes. Dry this.

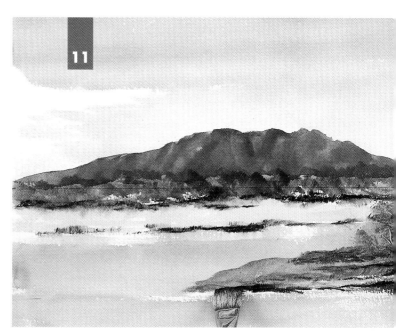

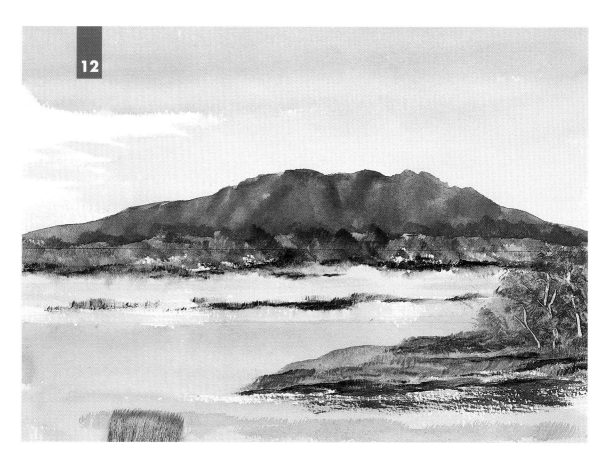

13 For the rocks, use a rigger and mix Cobalt blue with Raw sienna. Now paint in two little mounds with straight bases at the waterline.

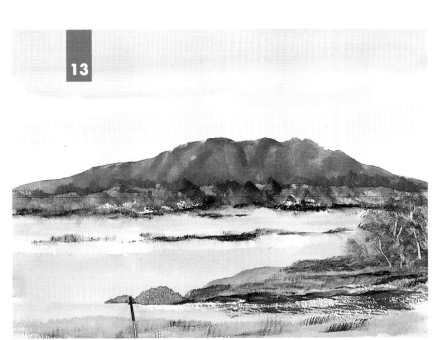

14 Use your dry large brush and neat Burnt umber, and paint in downward strokes to add some dark, dried grass along the near riverbank.

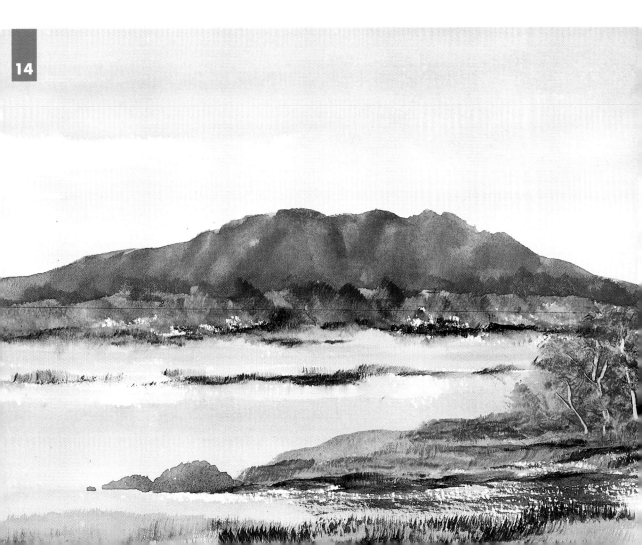

ROLLING RIVER

Add Joe, the bird, flying high
in the sky with a little Burnt
umber on your rigger. Sign your
painting and that's it, the rolling
Rio Grande!

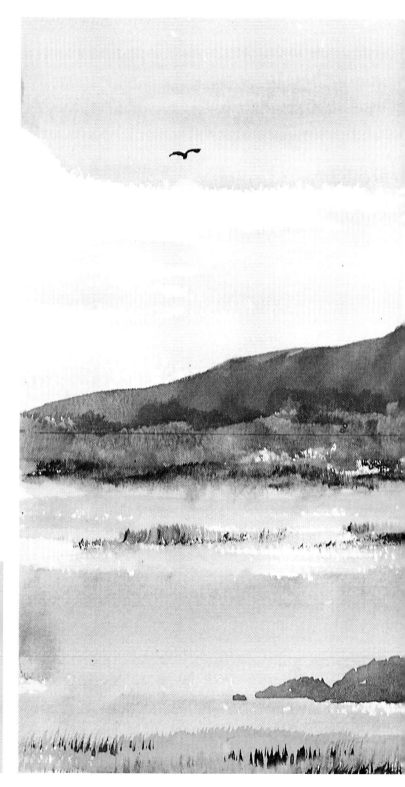

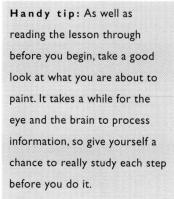

Handy tip: As well as
reading the lesson through
before you begin, take a good
look at what you are about to
paint. It takes a while for the
eye and the brain to process
information, so give yourself a
chance to really study each step
before you do it.

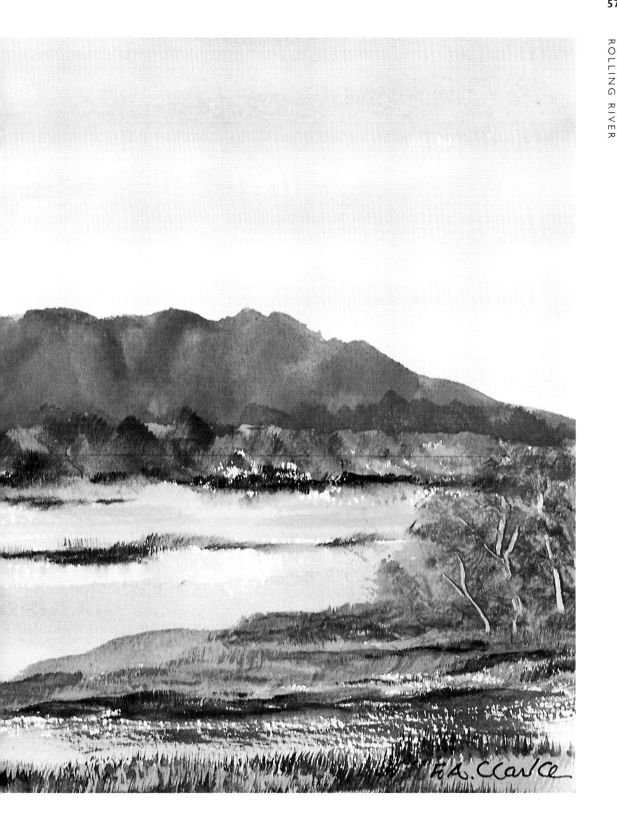

sea **fort**

This picture is from my travels to the old city of Caesarea in Israel, once one of the biggest ports on the Mediterranean, built by the Romans. If you need a headstart, look at pages 104–5 for help with drawing buildings.

you will need

- Paint: Cobalt blue, Lemon yellow, Raw sienna, Burnt umber, Light red and White gouache
- Brushes: your large (1½-inch) brush, small (¾-inch) brush and no.3 rigger (also an old small brush to use with the masking fluid, if you have one)
- Paper: a sheet of 10 × 14-inch (255 × 355-mm) 140lb/300gsm watercolour paper

- Palette (your white plate or tray)
- Water pot
- Cloths
- Pencil and ruler
- Eraser
- Board: 16 × 20 inches (410 × 508 mm) to stick your paper on
- Masking tape to stick the paper onto the board
- Masking fluid
- Hairdryer, if you have one

1

1 HORIZON Using masking tape across the corners, fix your sheet of paper lengthways onto your board. With a pencil, draw the horizon line about half way up the paper. Prop up the board.

2 Buildings are just boxes. Look closely at my example then start in the centre of the page with the main tower. Work across to the right, drawing lines only (no fine detail), a box at a time, and compare how big or small the next is in relation to the last. Add the arches, just letter 'u's upside down, then add the rocks.

3 Use your old brush and masking fluid (see page 29 for advice) to cover the buildings and rocks below. Dry this thoroughly.

4 SKY With your large brush, mix Cobalt blue with some water. Paint down to the horizon line, over the buildings, adding more water to lighten the sky as you go down the paper. Dry this.

5 MIDDLEGROUND With the small brush, mix Cobalt blue with a tiny bit of Lemon yellow. Draw a guideline for the beach edge, then paint from right to left, from the horizon, down the page. Add a bit more yellow to create the slightly greener, shallower water.

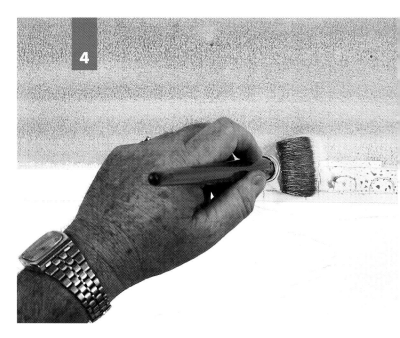

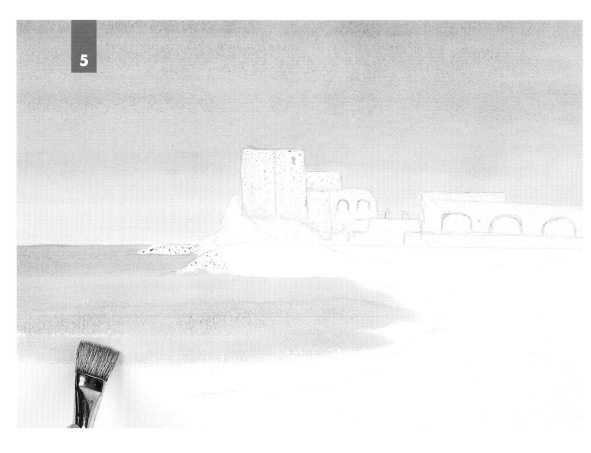

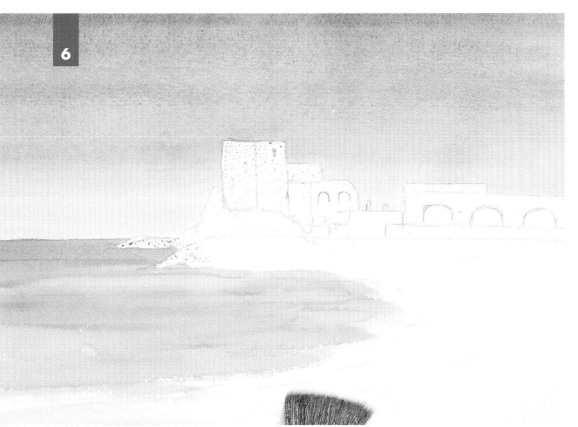

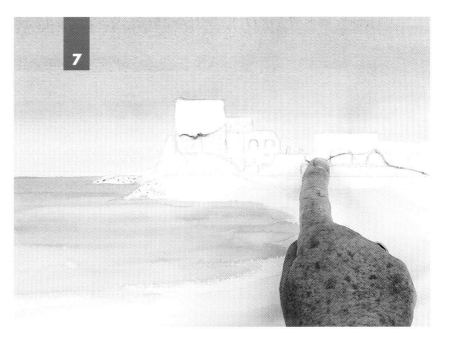

6 For the beach, use your large brush and a weak mix of Raw sienna with a little Burnt umber. Leave a white gap at the shoreline and paint in several curves of sand. While wet, darken the paint with a touch more Burnt umber and add further curves to fill in the beach. Dry this.

7 Carefully remove the masking fluid with a clean finger or eraser. Rub towards the centre of the buildings.

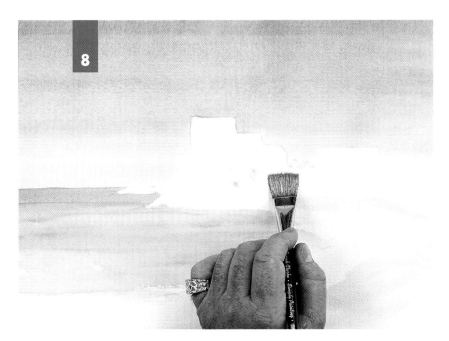

8 With your small brush, make a watery mix of Raw sienna and a tiny bit of Light red. Paint the buildings and top rocks. Dry this.

9 With your rigger, mix some Light red, Burnt umber and a tiny bit of Cobalt blue, and fill in the shaded (right) sides of the fort buildings using downward strokes.

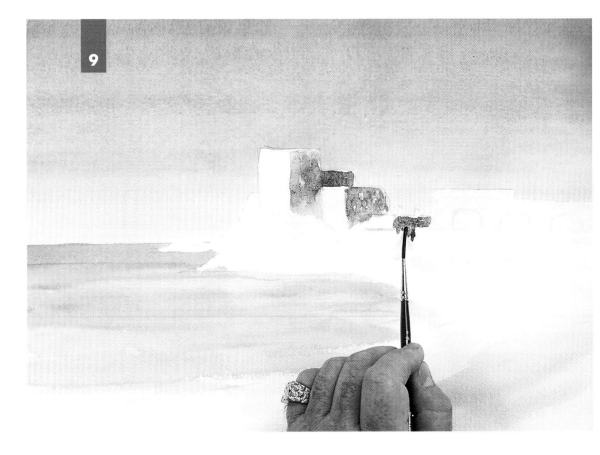

10 Finish the shading across the building tops. With your small brush, add a little water to your shadow paint mix and fill in the bit of the fort that leads down to the beach (below the arched section) and the middle of the rocky outcrop. Dry this. Mix a darkish colour from Light red and Cobalt blue and paint the tops of the rocks below the main tower on their shaded, right sides. Add more Light red and dab in the lower rocks at the edge of the beach. Dry this.

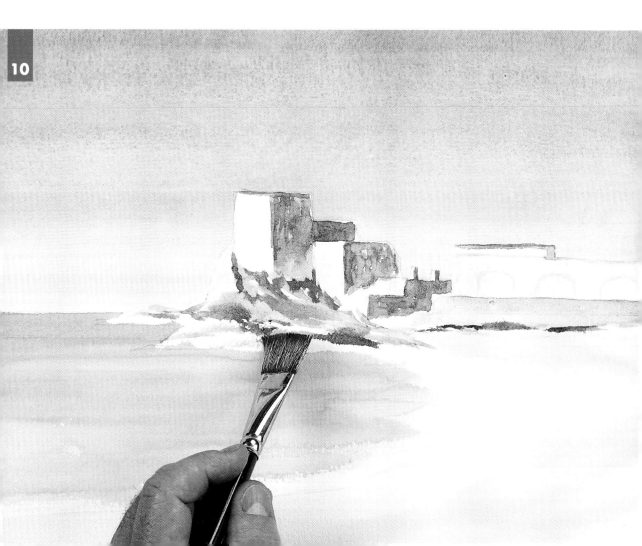

11 With your rigger, darken patches of the other rocks with your purplish mix of Light red and Cobalt blue. The big windows are Cobalt blue with Burnt umber. The smaller main-tower windows are paler and created with a single vertical brushstroke.

12 The arches are filled with a mix of pale Burnt umber and a bit of Cobalt blue. Dry this. Add more of the same colours to the mix to darken it, and shade the left sides of the arches.

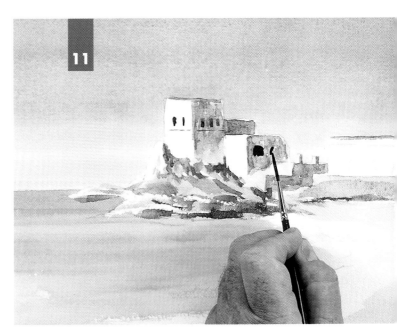

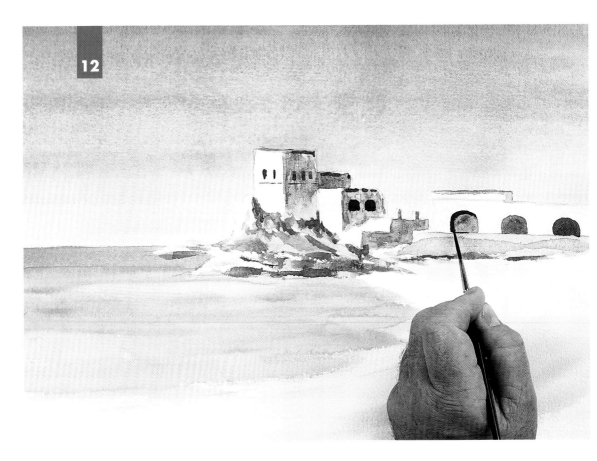

13 FOREGROUND For the waves, use your rigger and white gouache mixed with water. Start at the top with lines by the horizon then follow the line of the shore in curves.

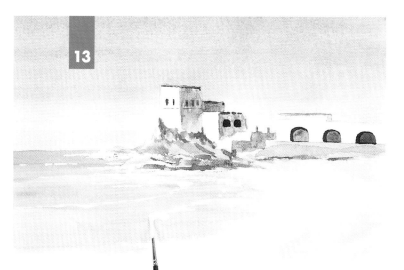

14 Darken the shoreline with some watery Burnt umber on your rigger, to show bits of seaweed and little rocks. If any look too harsh, a clean brush with a little water brushed over the area will help to soften the colour and blend the edges into the surrounding sand.

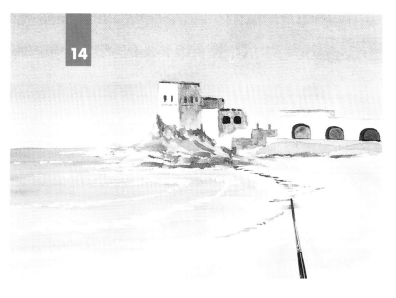

15 Add two carrot people to scale in Burnt umber (one with a Raw sienna shirt) and add their speckled shadows. Add further very pale Burnt umber patches to the sand to show the ups and downs. Add some seagulls wheeling to the left of the sea fort in white gouache.

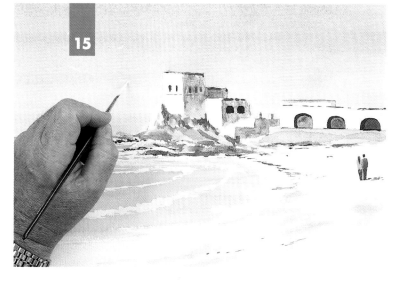

SEA FORT

When I finished this picture,
I noticed that the dark line on
top, left side of my main tower
looked a little bit harsh, so I've
taken a bit of very watery white
gouache on my rigger to soften
it a little. I've also straightened up
the left wall of the tower. You
can do this, too – go back to an
area you're not happy with and
make small corrections … but
don't mess about too much!
Don't forget to sign and frame
your painting.

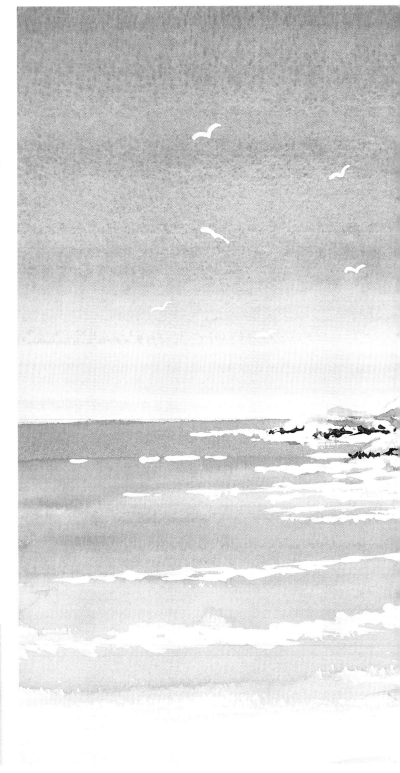

Handy tip: Practise drawing
your buildings so you know
how to build up the boxes and
shapes before you start your
painting. See pages 104–5 for
some help if you need it.

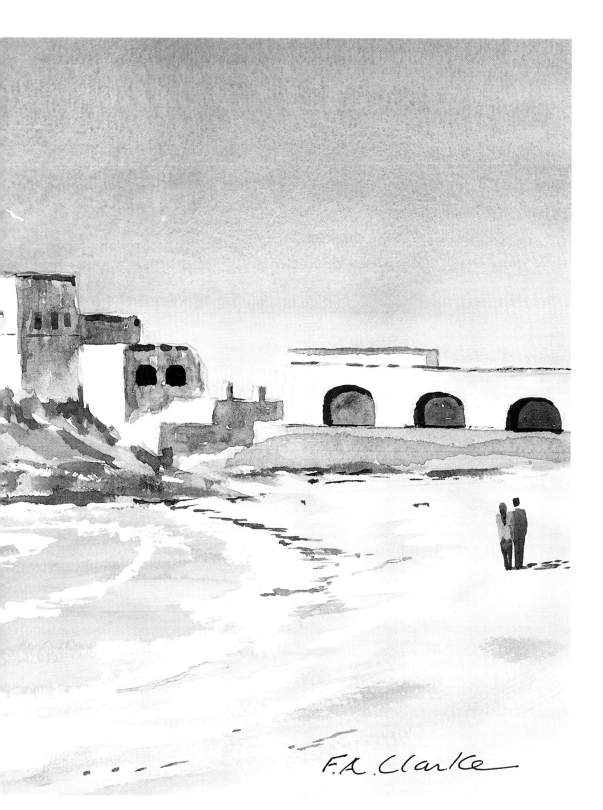

F.A. Clarke

wild **sunset**

It's usually when we're on holiday that we have time to watch the sun set, and to paint for that matter. When the sky turns unusual colours it can be quite dramatic, wild and bold, like the sunset in this painting.

you will need

- Paint: Lemon yellow, Alizarin crimson, Ultramarine blue, Burnt umber and White gouache
- Brushes: your large (1½-inch) brush and no.3 rigger (also an old small brush to use with the masking fluid, if you have one)
- Paper: a sheet of 10 × 14-inch (255 × 355-mm) 140lb/300gsm watercolour paper
- Palette (your white plate or tray)
- Water pot
- Cloths

- Pencil
- Ruler
- Eraser
- Board: 16 × 20 inches (410 × 508 mm) to stick your paper on
- Masking tape to stick the paper onto the board
- Masking fluid
- Coin or similar circular object (smooth-edged and about 1¼ inches/3 cm across)
- Hairdryer, if you have one

1

1 HORIZON Using masking tape across the corners, fix your sheet of paper lengthways onto your board. With a pencil, draw the horizon line about 2½ inches (6.5 cm) up from the paper's bottom edge. Prop up the board.

2 SKY Draw around your coin with a pencil to form a sun 2 inches (5 cm) above the horizon. Fill it in with masking fluid – paint just outside the pencil line then you can rub it out later when you remove the fluid. Dry this.

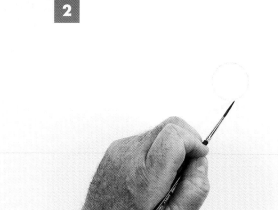

3 Put Lemon yellow, Alizarin crimson and Ultramarine blue out on your palette. Use your large brush, wet it, and dip it into the Lemon yellow. Paint a couple of broad horizontal strokes over your sun, from just above to just below it. While it's wet …

4 Clean the brush and mix Alizarin crimson with water. Paint broad strokes across the top of the sky, leaving some yellow untouched, and continue below the sun to just above the horizon line. While it's wet …

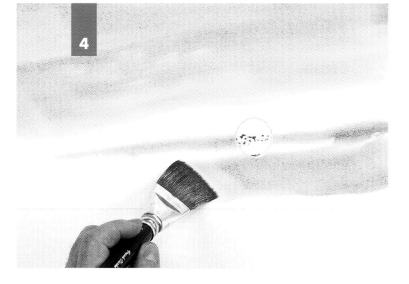

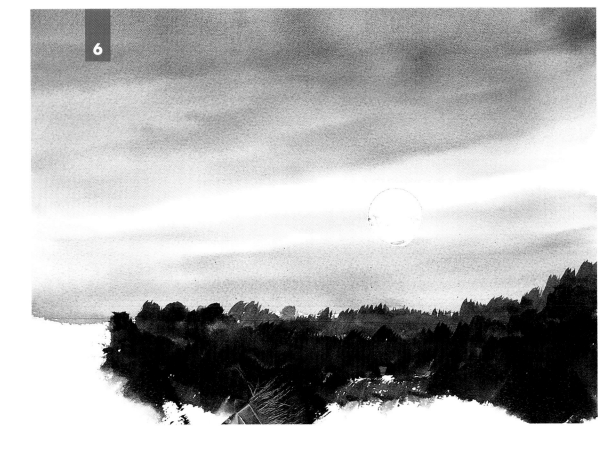

5 Mix Ultramarine blue with water and, starting from the top, paint down towards the sun. The effect is that the sky turns a purplish colour. Add a little more water and sweep in a little more paler blue under the sun. Don't go overboard and don't fiddle! Dry this.

6 MIDDLEGROUND AND FOREGROUND For ease, these have become one. Still using a fairly dry large brush, mix Alizarin crimson, Ultramarine blue and Burnt umber to make a deep wine colour. Use it almost neat and make plenty of it. In this step we will be putting on layers of paint, which get darker as you build them up. Use the brush corner and dab in some distant bushes along the horizon line. Dry this. Dab in another layer of bushes in front and slightly below the top of these. Dry this, then add a little more Alizarin crimson to your brush and touch over some parts of the bushes.

7 Use the same wine paint mix and the large brush corner, fairly dry then loaded with the paint, to lightly dab in the trees on the left, from bottom to top. Let the sky behind show through in patches. Dry this.

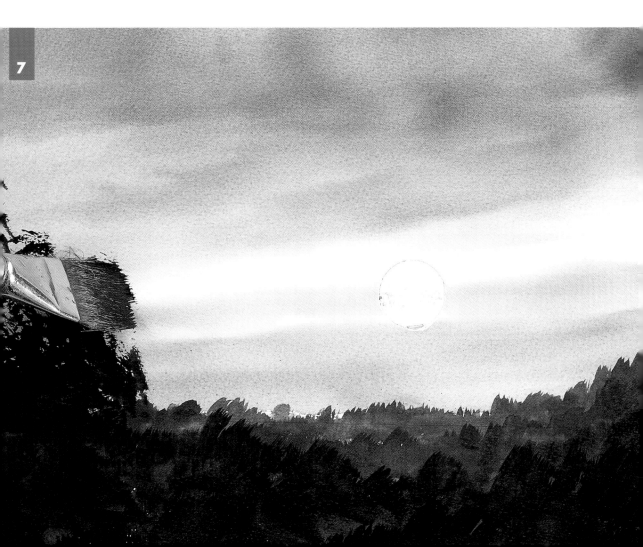

7

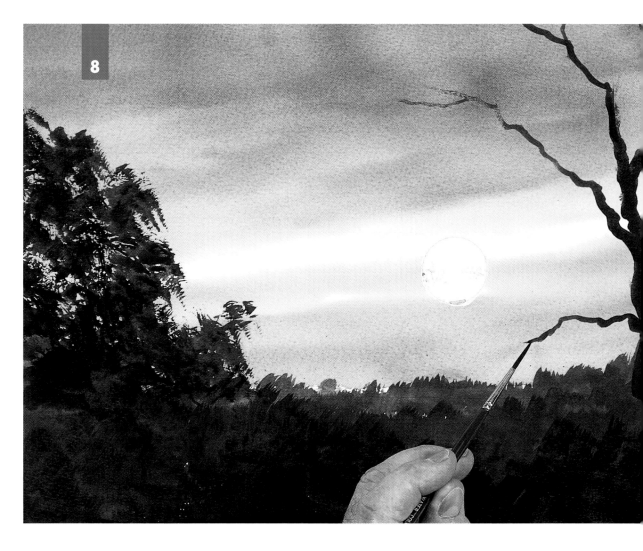

8 Use your rigger and take some of your wine paint mix and add a little neat Burnt umber to it. Paint in the tree trunk and branches on the right. Dry this.

9 With a dry large brush and more of the wine paint mix, lightly stipple the bristle tips along the branches to form some leaves. Don't go mad – you want to see the sky behind!

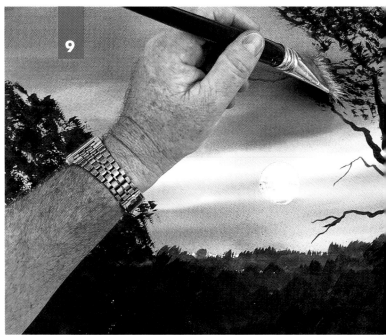

10 With your rigger, add some stray branches to the trees on the left with the Burnt umber version of your wine paint mix (that you made in step 8).

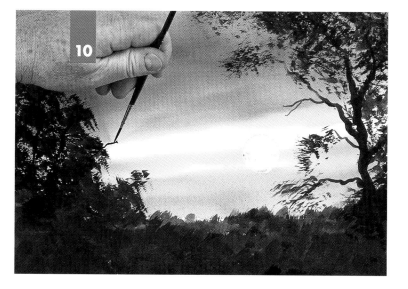

11 To create a slightly glowing effect on the top of the foliage underneath the sun, with a clean, dry, large brush mix Lemon yellow and a tiny bit of Alizarin crimson. Stipple this over the central area of foliage top. Dry this then add a little neat Lemon yellow to highlight a few areas.

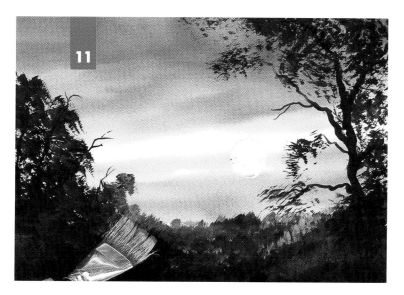

12 Remove the masking fluid from the sun, rubbing towards the centre. With your rigger, mix Alizarin crimson and Ultramarine blue with water to match the pink colour of the sky (test it on a scrap of paper) and gently paint a couple of lines across the face of the sun.

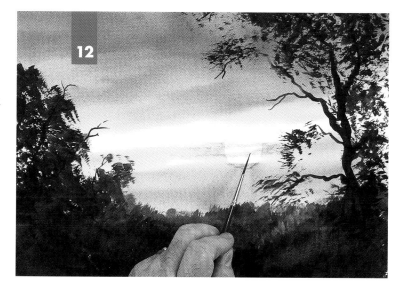

WILD SUNSET

Well done! Add your bird above the treetops on the left with some dark wine paint, then sign off in white gouache this time.

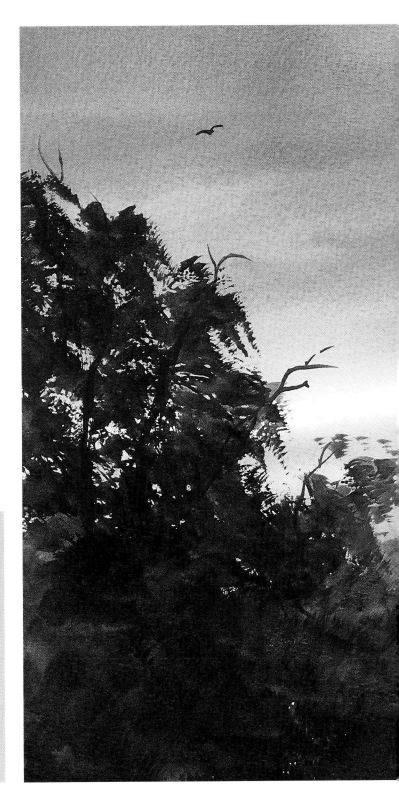

Handy tip: Try to mix up enough of the colour you're using as it can be tricky trying to recreate the same colour mix again. Reading a lesson through before you start will help you see how much of a particular mix you might need. If you find you do need to mix more, always test the mix on a scrap of paper to be sure you're happy with it.

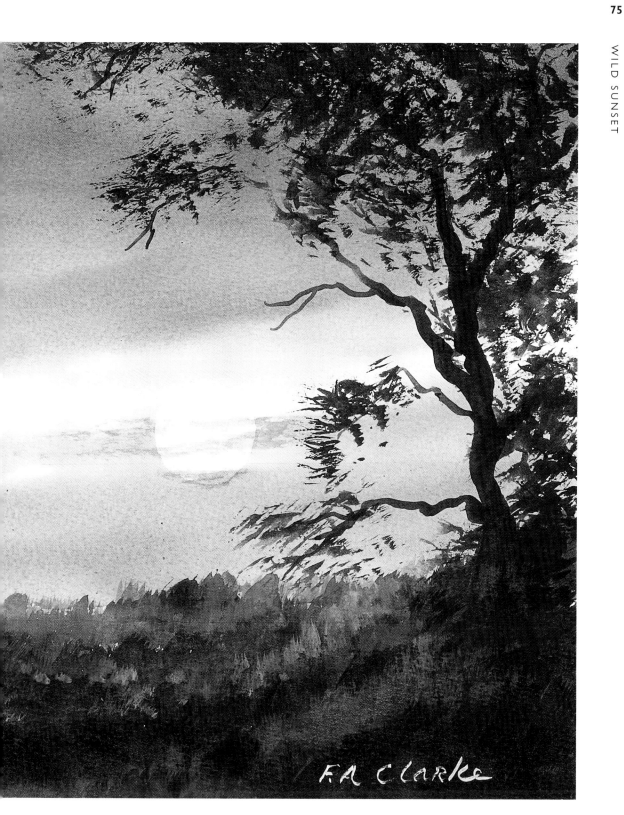

F.A Clarke

tumbling **falls**

This painting is of Ennistymon Falls, probably the most famous waterfall in Ireland and the most painted. Take your time. The houses are easy – just lines and boxes. Try drawing a simple house like the one below or take a look at pages 104–5 to give you confidence in drawing buildings.

you will need

- Paint: Raw sienna, Ultramarine blue, Light red, Burnt umber, and Lemon yellow
- Brushes: your large (1½-inch) brush, small (¾-inch) brush and no.3 rigger (also an old small brush to use with the masking fluid, if you have one)
- Paper: a sheet of 10 × 14-inch (255 × 355-mm) 140lb/300gsm watercolour paper

- Palette (your white plate or tray)
- Water pot
- Cloths
- Pencil and ruler
- Eraser
- Board: 16 × 20 inches (410 × 508 mm) to stick your paper on
- Masking tape to stick the paper onto the board
- Masking fluid
- Hairdryer, if you have one

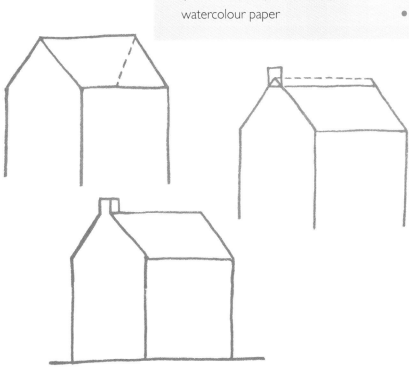

Handy tip: When drawing buildings into a landscape, always start with the main one in the centre of the group and work out to the edge of the page. That way, if you have miscalculated their size you can just leave out the end ones. Practise drawing a single house, like this, before you get started on the row of houses needed for the painting project.

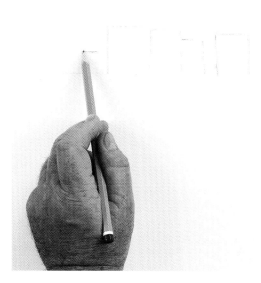

1 HORIZON Using masking tape across the corners, fix your sheet of paper upright onto your board. With a pencil, draw the horizon line in the centre, about 7½ inches (19 cm) up from the paper's bottom edge. Prop up the board.

2 For the houses, draw five boxes along the horizon line. Do this freehand, not with a ruler!

3 Add the roofs (just slanting rectangles), some small boxes on top for the chimneys (see page 105 for a reminder) and add the sides of the houses. Cover the roofs and the top parts of the buildings with masking fluid and dry this thoroughly.

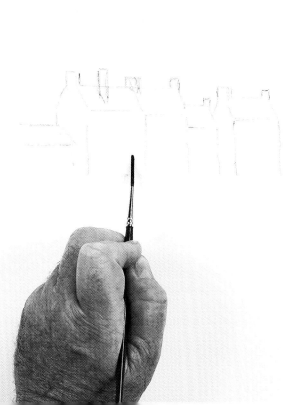

4 SKY Put out Raw sienna, Ultramarine blue and Light red on your palette. With the large brush, mix the Raw sienna with water and paint it in broad horizontal strokes over the entire sky area. While wet, mix some Ultramarine blue with water and, from the top, paint most of the sky area, leaving some Raw sienna showing through. Again, while wet, use 50% Ultramarine blue with 50% Light red and sweep in darker patches in the top half of the sky. Dry this.

5 MIDDLEGROUND AND FOREGROUND For the steps of the falls, draw five light pencil lines in below the horizon line, getting slightly further apart and longer as you move down the page. With your small brush mix Ultramarine blue with a little Light red. Use the flat chisel edge of the brush and paint over your top pencil line. Dry the brush a little, add paint and drag down in slightly bowed, diagonal, strokes almost down to the next line, leaving white patches (to represent the foam). Paint four cascades in this way.

6 Paint the fifth water line and some tumbling water on the left side only (if my hand's too much in the way in the picture here, step 8 on page 80 shows this part of the painting more clearly!). Use horizontal brush strokes to form the flat river water at the base of the falls. For the right-hand trees, use a fairly dry large brush and a mix of neat Raw sienna and Light red and dab in the back layer of trees. While wet, add more Light red with a little Ultramarine blue mixed in for the second layer. While wet …

7 Add some neat Burnt umber at the tree bases and scratch in the trunks with a fingernail. Dry this. Take more Raw sienna with Light red and dab in some bushes at the second cascade level. Dry this then mix Lemon yellow with a little Ultramarine blue to paint the greener centre of the bushes. Stipple in some darker areas in Burnt umber and paint a line of shadow at the base. Finally, touch a little Light red to the green bush to show where the leaves are just turning.

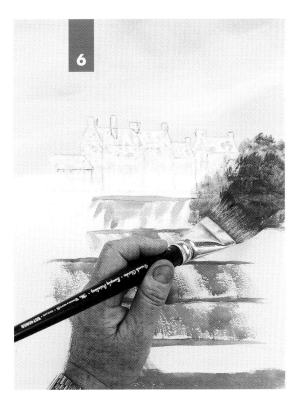

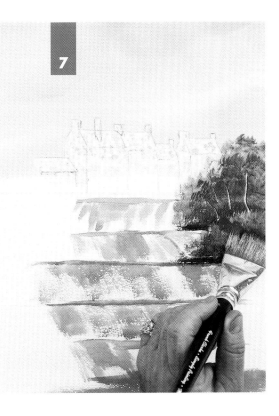

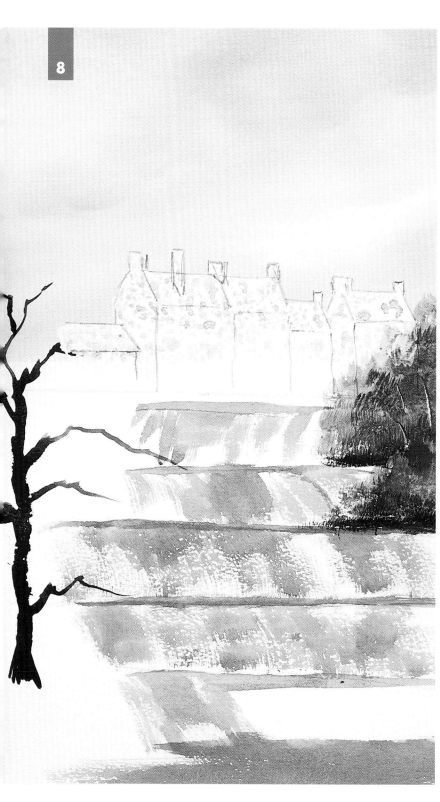

8 Use Burnt umber on your rigger to paint the main trunk and branches of the tree.

9 For the foliage, use an almost dry large brush and dab the mix of Raw sienna and Light red lightly along the branches. Add more Light red with a little Ultramarine blue to darken the mix and paint the second layer of leaves. Touch some Burnt umber around the tree base. Dry this.

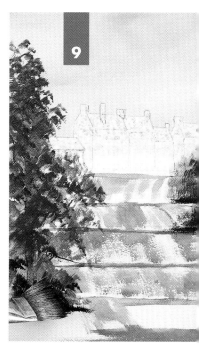

10 Rub off the masking fluid, rubbing towards its centre. For the roofs, start at their tops and work in downward strokes with your rigger using varying colours: Burnt umber with Ultramarine blue creates dark slate, and add water to get a paler grey.

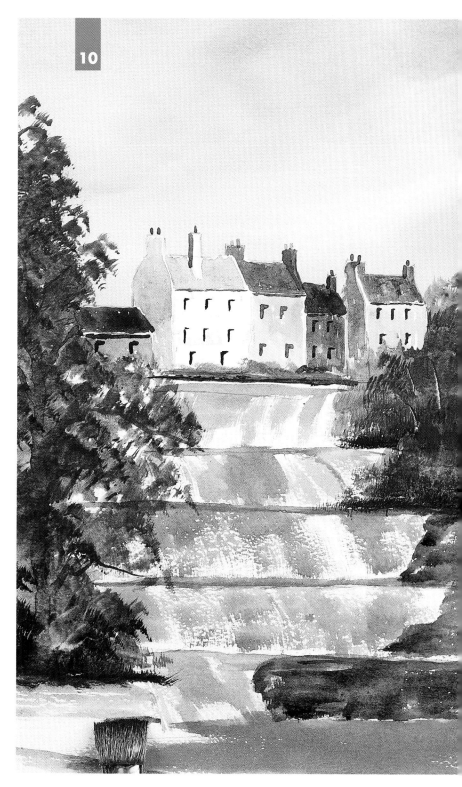

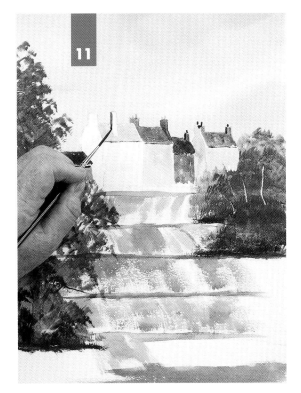

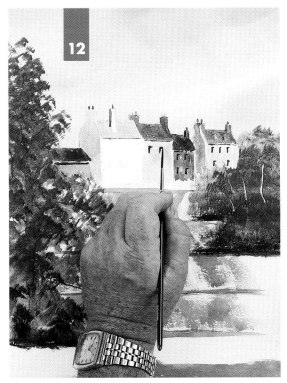

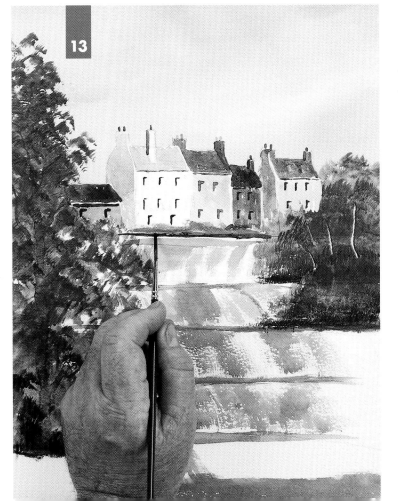

11 For the browner roofs, use Burnt umber neat or mixed with Raw sienna. Dry this. For the walls, you can use any colours you like really. I've used various mixes, starting from the right-hand side: house 1 is a pale Light red and Raw sienna, house 2 is Burnt umber and Light red, house 3 is Lemon yellow and Raw sienna, house 4 I've left white and house 5 is Ultramarine blue and Burnt umber. Once painted, dry the houses.

12 Mix Burnt umber and Ultramarine blue and paint lines for roof-edge gutters. The chimney shading is a mix of Light red and Ultramarine blue. For the windows, use your mix of Burnt umber and Ultramarine blue and paint upside down 'L's.

13 For the riverbank below the houses mix Lemon yellow and a tiny bit of Ultramarine blue and paint in a line of green with your rigger. Dry this. Now add some Raw sienna to the mix and dab in a second layer. Add a little Burnt umber to define the edge of the bank.

14 To shape and paint in the rock shelves on the right, use the small brush and mix Light red and Ultramarine blue. For the left shelf, lightly paint in two stripes of Raw sienna mixed with a little Burnt umber.

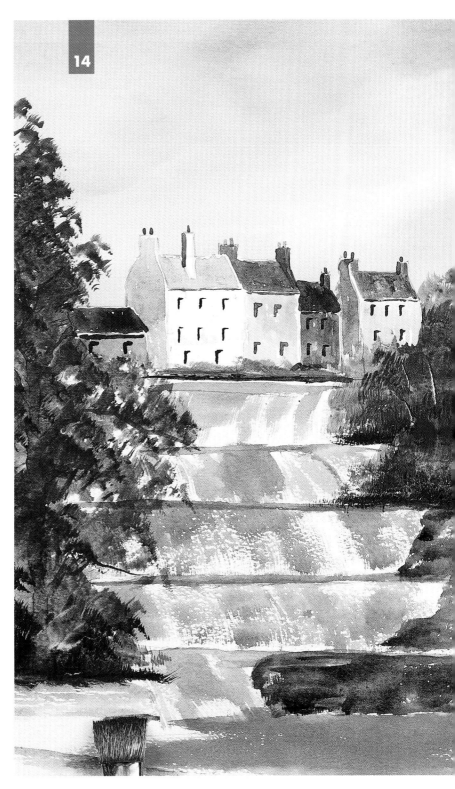

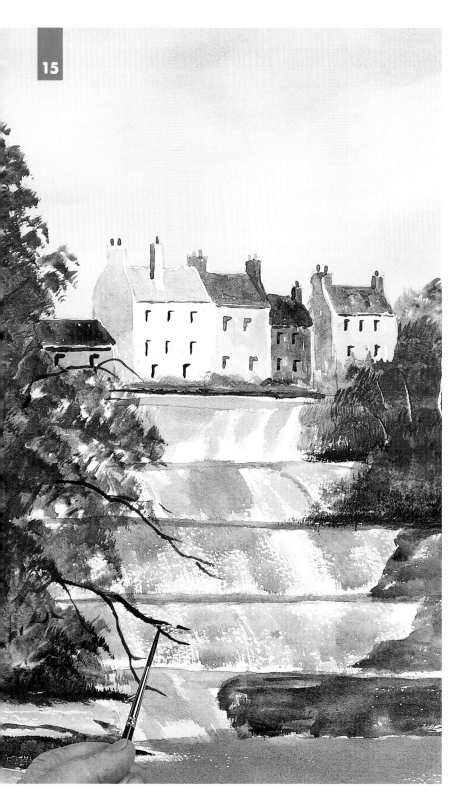

15 Darken this slightly with Ultramarine blue and Burnt umber and, with downward strokes of a fairly dry brush, fill in the left shelf area. Dry this. Use the rigger and some Burnt umber to add a few stray branches to your big tree. Dry this.

TUMBLING FALLS

Mix some Raw sienna with some Light red and, with a dry large brush, dab it carefully along the ends of some of the branches. Add Joe in Burnt umber, high above your houses, and sign your tumbling falls.

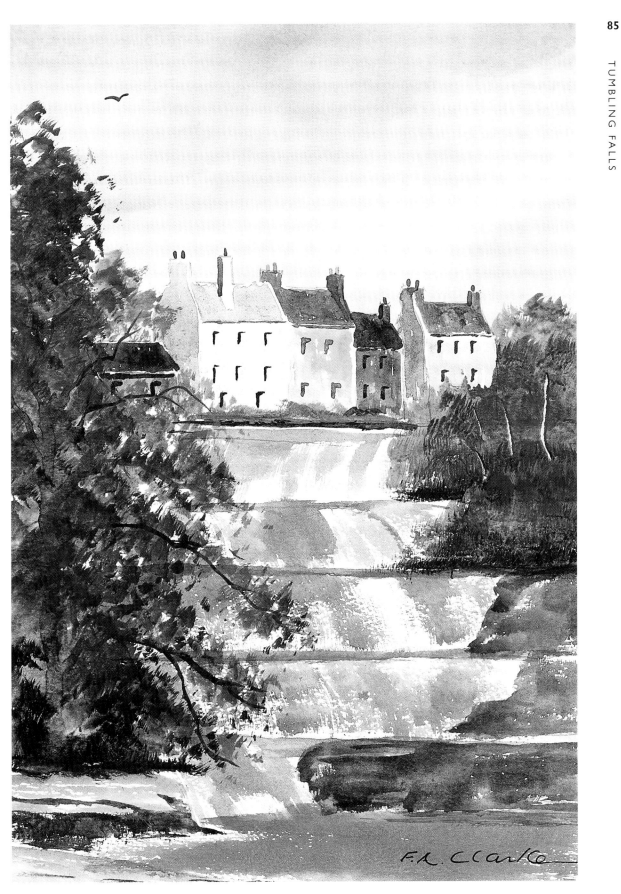

F.h.Clarke

little **orchard**

This is a great tree-painting exercise. Practise a few before you start if you like (see page 19 for a reminder). We are painting from the distance towards the foreground and each tree's paint mix is just a darker version of the one that went before. It's easy – let me show you.

you will need

- Paint: Ultramarine blue, Lemon yellow, Raw sienna, Burnt umber, Alizarin crimson and White gouache
- Brushes: your large (1½-inch) brush, small (¾-inch) brush and no.3 rigger
- Paper: a sheet of 10 × 14-inch (255 × 355-mm) 140lb/300gsm watercolour paper

- Palette (your white plate or tray)
- Water pot
- Cloths
- Pencil and ruler
- Eraser
- Board: 16 × 20 inches (410 × 508 mm) to stick your paper on
- Masking tape to stick the paper onto the board
- Hairdryer, if you have one

1

1 HORIZON Using masking tape across the corners, fix your sheet of paper lengthways onto your board. With a pencil, draw the horizon line about 4¾ inches (12 cm) up from the paper's bottom edge. Prop up the board.

2 SKY With your large brush, mix Ultramarine blue with lots of water and paint in broad horizontal sweeps, down to the horizon line. Dry this.

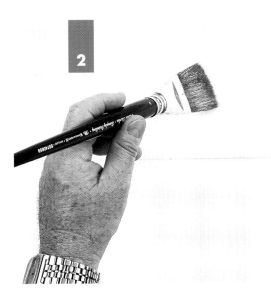

3 MIDDLEGROUND Make a watery 50/50 mix of Lemon yellow with Raw sienna and paint in the entire area below the horizon. Dry this.

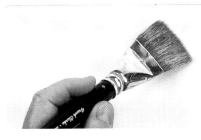

4 Mix more pale Lemon yellow and Raw sienna with a tiny bit of Ultramarine blue. Paint a broken layer of pale green, moving across the page but using small downward strokes.

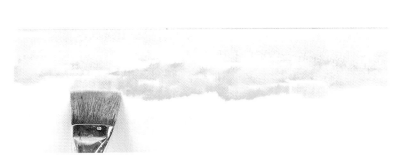

5 Add a tiny touch more Ultramarine blue as you come down the paper to form slightly darker grass to fill the foreground area. Dry this. Use your rigger and watery Raw sienna mixed with a touch of Burnt umber for the distant tree – keep the paint mix very pale. Dry this.

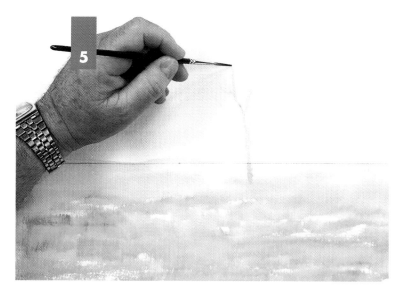

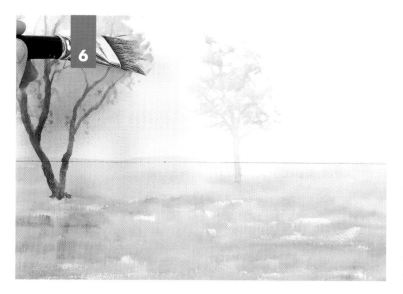

6 Mix Lemon yellow, Raw sienna and a touch of Ultramarine blue with water. Use the corner of a dry large brush and stipple in pale leaves on the distant tree. With your rigger, mix in a tiny bit more Burnt umber to your tree trunk mix and paint a second tree. Dry this. For its leaves use your Lemon yellow, Raw sienna and Ultramarine blue pale leaf mix and stipple it onto your second tree with a dry brush. Dry this.

7 Slightly darken your green mix with a touch of Ultramarine blue and stipple patches onto the second tree. Darken your tree trunk mix by adding a touch of Raw Sienna and Burnt Umber and, using your rigger, paint in a third tree. Dry this. Darken the right sides of the tree by adding more Burnt umber to the mix.

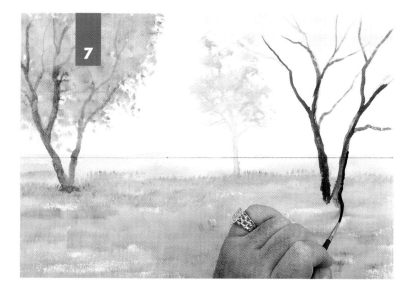

8 FOREGROUND Mix a touch more blue into your green mix and stipple a layer of leaves onto the third tree. Dry this. Darken the green paint again by adding a touch more Ultramarine blue and stipple on darker leaves. Add a touch of Burnt umber and dab in some downward strokes of grass with a dry large brush at the bases of the trees. Now take your rigger and darken your tree trunk mix again by adding more Raw sienna and Burnt umber to it. Now paint in your fourth tree. Dry this.

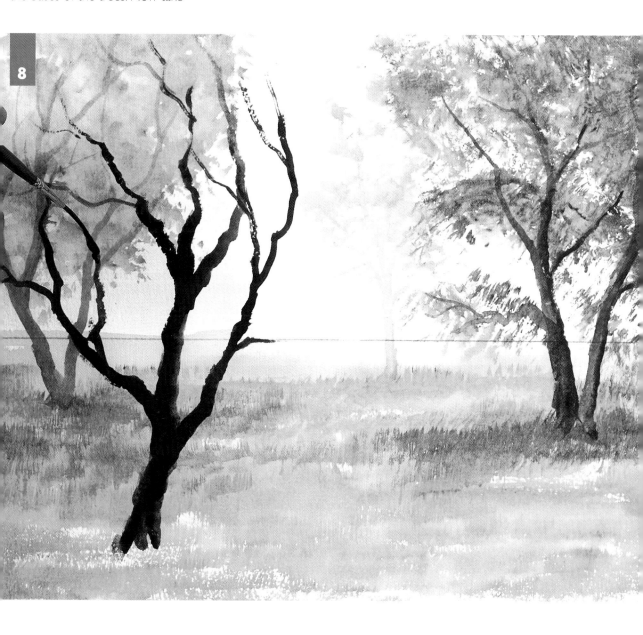

9 Use your darker green mix of Lemon yellow, Raw sienna and a touch of Ultramarine blue and stipple leaves along the fourth tree's branches with the corner of a dry large brush. Dry this.

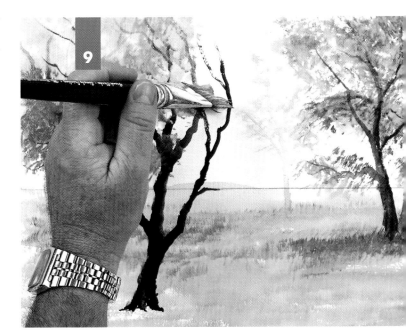

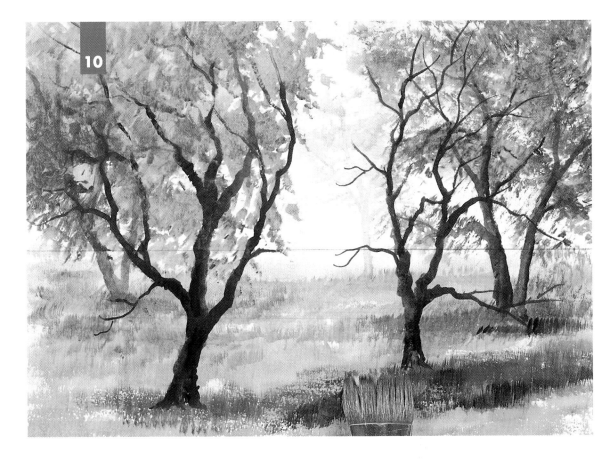

10 Add a touch more blue and stipple in a second darker layer of leaves on the fourth tree and some grass below the third and fourth trees. Use your rigger and almost pure Burnt umber for the fifth tree on the left. Dry this. Add further dark green grass and darken the paint with some Burnt umber to get shaded areas around its base.

11 Stipple the tiniest bit of pale foliage on the left branch tips of the fifth tree. Dry this.

For the daisies, paint four dots of White gouache close together using the tip of the rigger. For the poppies, mix Alizarin crimson with White gouache. You can mix Lemon yellow with White gouache for colour variation if you like. Dry the flowers. Add stalks to a few of the flowers nearest you using little downward strokes of Burnt umber, and add dark centres to a few of your flowers to finish them off.

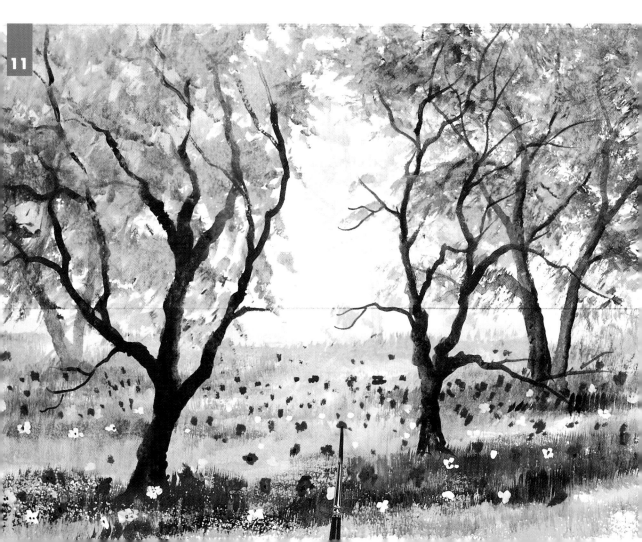

11

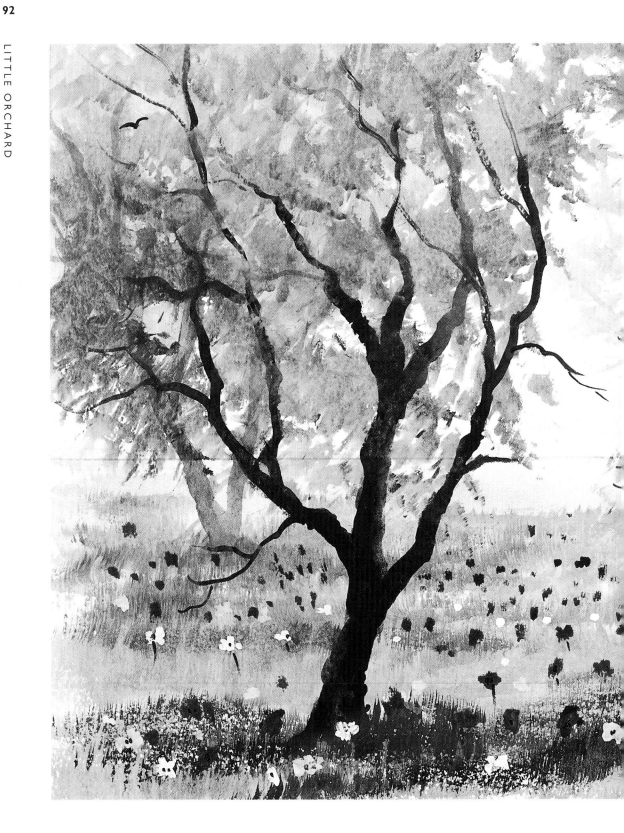

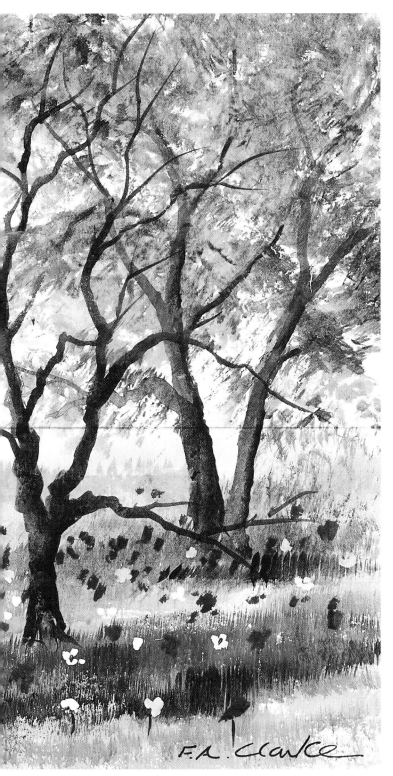

LITTLE ORCHARD

Can you see my bird in the treetops on the left? Sign your orchard and frame your masterpiece!

Handy tip: Usually, the further away the something is, the paler it is. You can give a sense of distance by using paler colours, as I've done here, in the background. The trees get darker and more detailed, the nearer they are to you.

snowy **slopes**

I was in Vermont, in America, when I saw the moon rise over a fresh fall of snow. It inspired me to paint this winter snow scene. It would make a great Christmas card – you could find a small, local printer and see if you can't get your painting printed up.

you will need

- Paint: Raw sienna, Cobalt blue, Payne's grey, Lemon yellow, Burnt umber and White gouache
- Brushes: your large (1½-inch) brush, small (¾-inch) brush and no.3 rigger (also an old small brush to use with the masking fluid, if you have one)
- Paper: a sheet of 10 × 14-inch (255 × 355-mm) 140lb/300gsm watercolour paper
- Palette (your white plate or tray)
- Water pot

- Cloths
- Pencil
- Ruler
- Eraser
- Board: 16 × 20 inches (410 × 508 mm) to stick your paper on
- Masking tape to stick the paper onto the board
- Masking fluid
- Coin or similar circular object (smooth-edged and about 1¼ inches/3 cm across)
- Hairdryer, if you have one

1

1 HORIZON Using masking tape across the corners, fix your sheet of paper lengthways onto your board. With a pencil, draw the horizon line about 4 inches (10 cm) up from the paper's bottom edge. Prop up the board.

2 SKY Draw around your coin to form a moon in your sky. Fill it in with masking fluid – paint just outside the line then you can rub it out later. Dry this. Put Raw sienna, Cobalt blue and Payne's grey on your palette. With your large brush, mix up some watery Raw sienna and paint in broad horizontal strokes, down to just above the horizon. While wet …

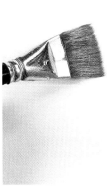

3 Clean the brush and quickly mix the Cobalt blue with a little Payne's grey and water – test it and make a fair bit as you'll be using it for more than the sky. Paint your blue-grey in diagonal strokes, going over the moon but leaving one or two sausage-shaped areas of Raw sienna showing through. Dry this.

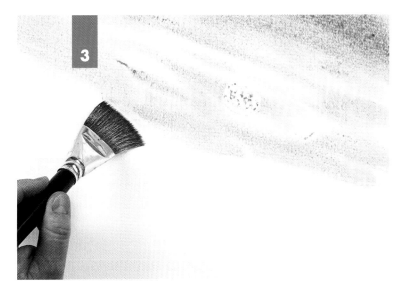

4 With the same blue-grey sky paint mix, paint in some mountains on the horizon line. (They are faint because it's a wintry day!) Dry this.

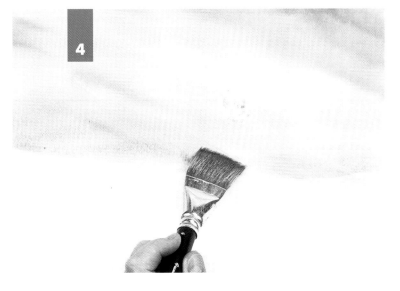

5 MIDDLEGROUND Start on the right-hand side and, still using the same blue-grey mix, add some shadows below the mountains to shape some hills and mounds of the snowscape.

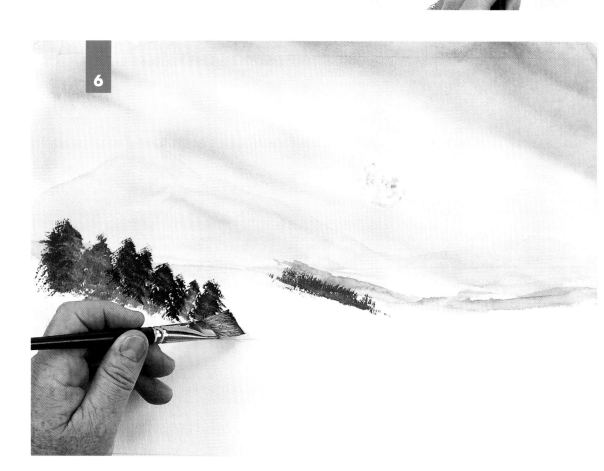

6 For the pine trees, mix Lemon yellow, Payne's grey and Cobalt blue with a little water for a dark green. Use the corner of a dry small brush and, in the distance, dab in a sloping area of trees. With the brush corner add a second area of larger trees — dab straight up from their bases to their pointed tips (see page 19 for a reminder). Start each a little further down the paper, running from left to right in a diagonal line, to give effect that they're standing on a slope. Dry this.

7 Again with your blue-grey sky mix on your small brush, continue the line of your slopes by dabbing them in (rather than painting a straight line) from left to right down the paper. Add a shaded area under the treeline and continue down the paper to give the impression of the slope in the foreground. Dry this.

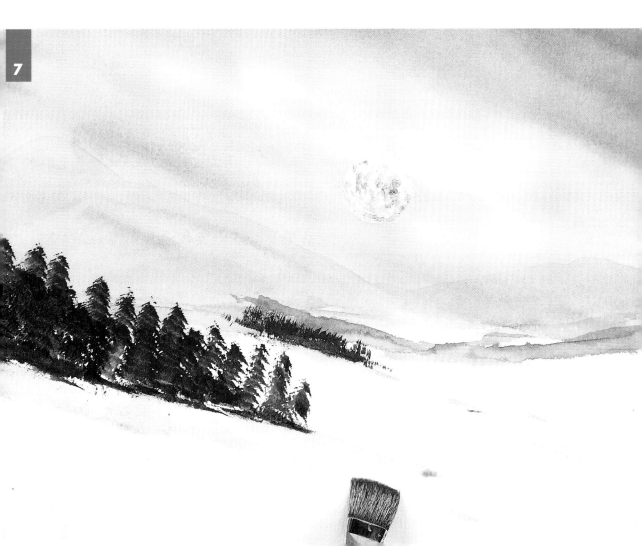

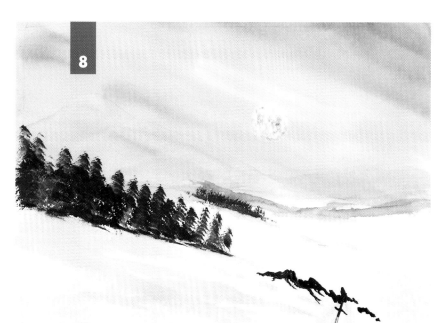

8 FOREGROUND For the rocks, use your rigger with a mix of Cobalt blue and Burnt umber. Start from the left and work down the page. Their bases won't be flat as snow will have stacked against them. Take your time and don't overdo them. Dry this.

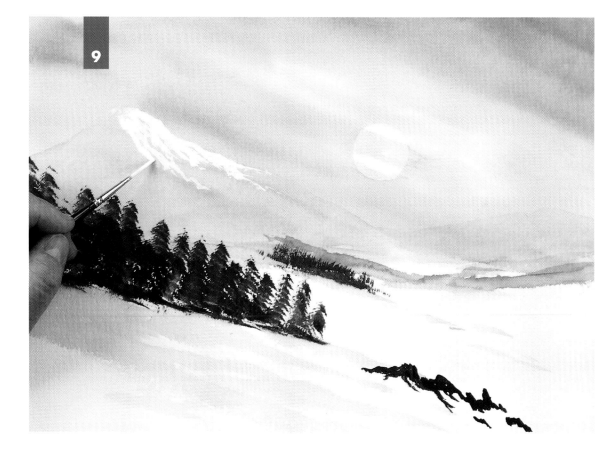

9 Rub the masking fluid off the moon towards its centre. Use your large brush and the blue-grey paint mix and, going in the same direction as your original sky strokes, lightly sweep across the face of the moon to leave a streak of blue. (You can leave the moon white if you want to.)

Moonlight will be shining on the right side of the mountain, so let's paint the snow-capped peak. Use your rigger with White gouache and follow the shape of the mountain, trailing thin wobbly lines down from the peak.

10 On the other side of the mountain peak, paint a more shaded snowy area by mixing some blue-grey sky paint into the White gouache. Let's add another little rock patch in Burnt umber and some tufts of grass in a Raw sienna with Burnt umber mix, poking through the melted snow.

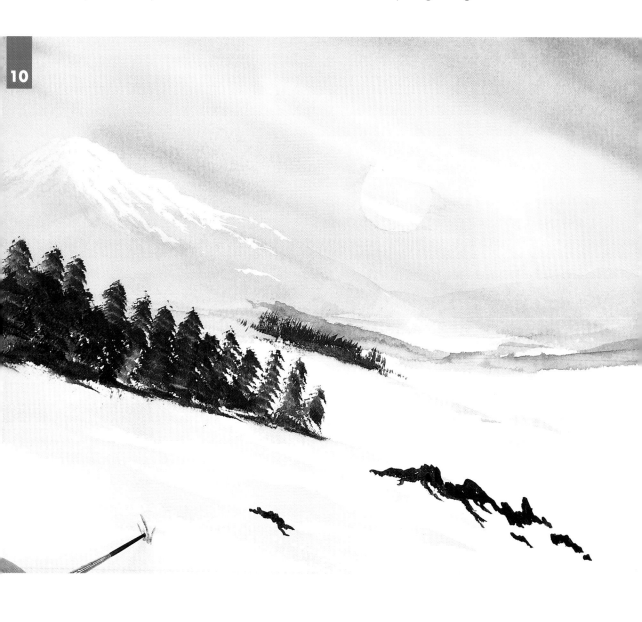

10

SNOWY SLOPES

Add your bird, in Burnt umber
with your rigger, over the
mountain and sign your picture.

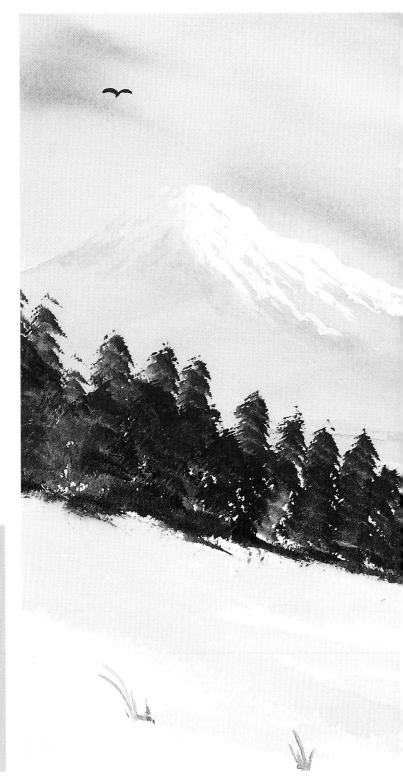

Handy tip: To make original
watercolour greeting cards, take
half a sheet of your paper
(measuring 10 × 7 inches/255 ×
175 mm). Tape it upright on your
board, divide the area in two
with a line halfway across and
paint a picture on the bottom
half of the paper. When you've
finished, fold it in half and you
have a unique, hand-painted card.

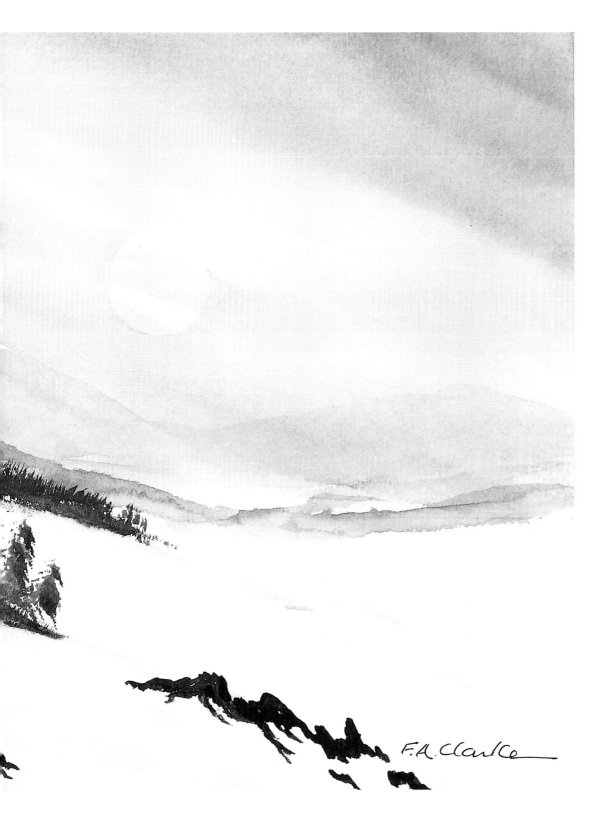

F.A.Clarke

using people for scale

I suppose it would be impossible for me to write a book without including my favourite vegetable, the carrot! Painting people is often seen as being too difficult but my carrots make it easy. Having them in a picture really helps to give a sense of scale to your painting. I'll just recap on how to paint carrot people for the newcomers then I'll show you how people and scale work.

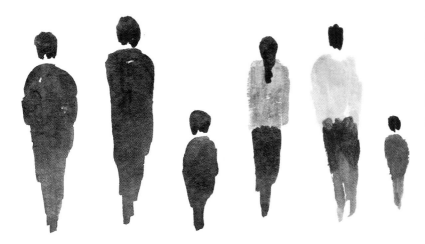

1 Get yourself a piece of paper and, using your rigger, paint the outline of a carrot and fill it in. Paint a blob on top for the head, leaving a tiny space to represent the person's neck.

2 Practise various sizes and embellish your carrots and soon you'll have them growing arms, legs and handbags. What these carrot people show, though, is that the smaller you paint them the further away they look in relation to each other. That's scale!

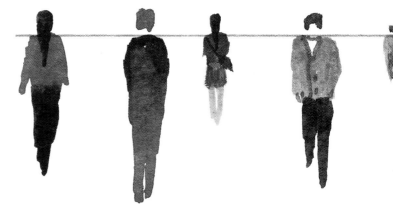

Handy tip: If you paint your figure wearing red, it will catch a viewer's eye and encourage people to look at your picture. You never know – they might like it enough to buy it!

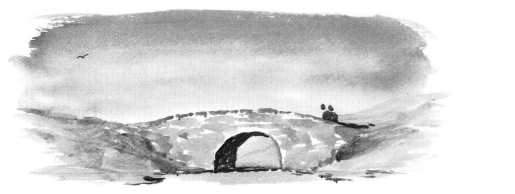

Using figures in a landscape can help show the scale of things like the rocks, trees or, in this case, the bridge. The bigger you make the people, the smaller the bridge seems to be.

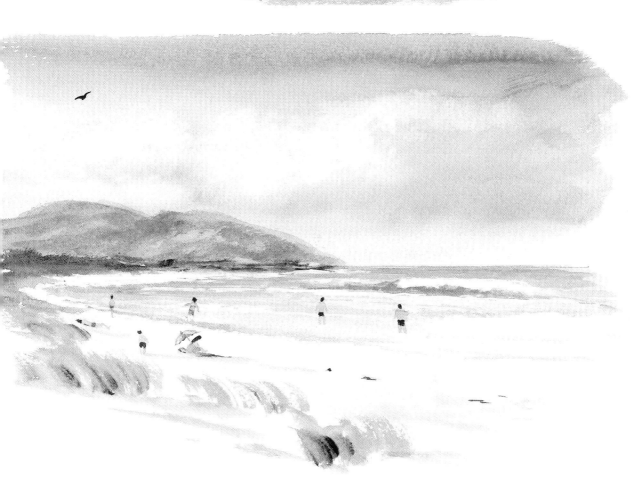

help with buildings, perspective and shadows

Seems silly to say this, but there is only one sun, so when you paint your pictures you should bear this in mind! Light will come from only one direction, to make one side of an object or building lighter and throw the other side into shadow. Here I want to show you how light, shadows and perspective can work to give realistic cottages, and then I'll show you how to simplify a complicated building like a castle which, when painted, really uses shadows to good effect.

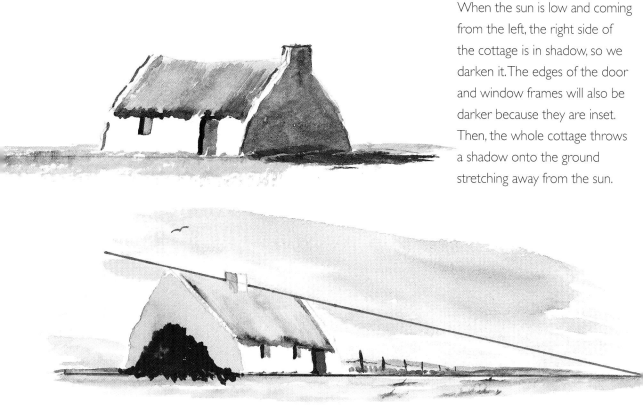

When the sun is low and coming from the left, the right side of the cottage is in shadow, so we darken it. The edges of the door and window frames will also be darker because they are inset. Then, the whole cottage throws a shadow onto the ground stretching away from the sun.

Perspective is about how things appear in relation to each other and according to their distance from the viewer. If an object like my cottage here is perched on the horizon line, with its roof getting smaller on one side, it gives the impression that the left side of the cottage is closest to the viewer with the right side further away in the distance. Draw in two faint guidelines to help you keep your perspective realistic.

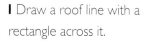

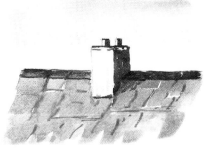

1 Draw a roof line with a rectangle across it.

2 Add another box to one side and join the base of this to the base of the rectangle.

3 Add smoke stacks (boxes). Paint the roof and chimney stack. By shading the right sides of the chimney and stacks, and a patch of roof to its right, we can bring the chimney to life.

Any building is just made up of different shaped boxes. Break the castle down into boxes of various heights: start in the middle and work away to the edges. Add uneven tops. When painted the shading gives it shape and depth.

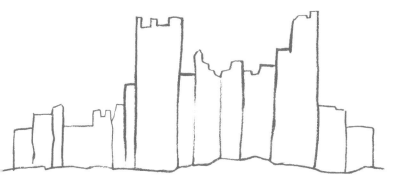

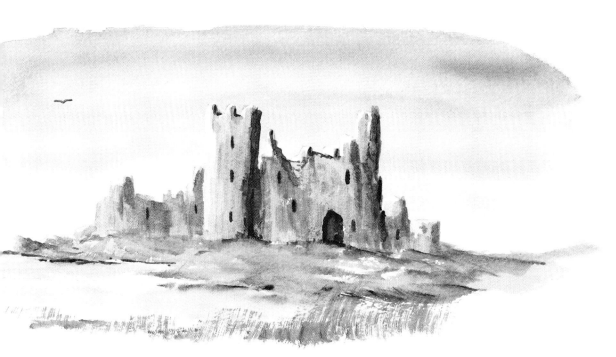

advice on simplifying boats

Drawing boats, like everthing else, can be simplified. Sailboats are really easy, and even a detailed rowboat can be broken down into simple shapes and curves. Follow the instructions and I'll have you sailing away in no time!

1 Draw a horizon line with a rectangle on it.

2 Draw two lines for the main mast, up from the centre of your rectangle to meet at the top. Add two parallel lines out from the lower end of the mast to form the boom. The sail is just two slightly curved lines to form a simple triangle shape. You can shape the sides of your rectangle to round out the boat hull before you paint it, if you like.

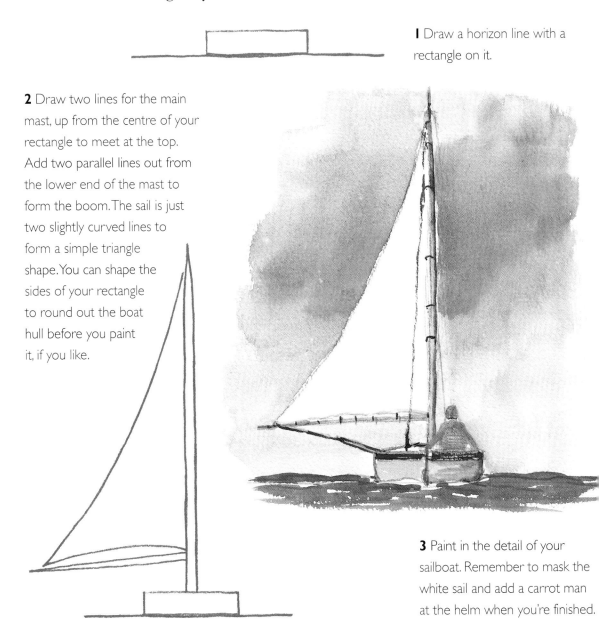

3 Paint in the detail of your sailboat. Remember to mask the white sail and add a carrot man at the helm when you're finished.

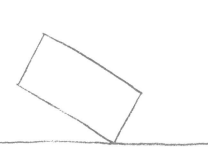

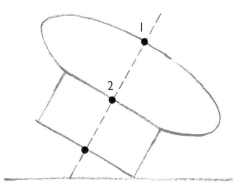

1 Draw a horizontal baseline then perch a tilted rectangle on it.

2 Draw a dotted line up through the rectangle. Draw an oval to join points 1 and 2 on both sides.

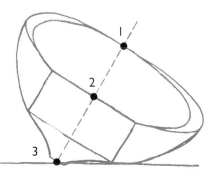

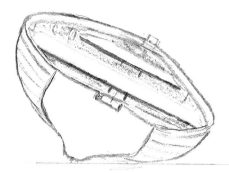

3 Draw another two curves, starting at point 1 and going outside the first oval then joining it. Draw two more curves to touch the rectangle's corners, and on down to shape the boat's bottom at point 3.

4 Shape the back panel of the boat, rounding the corners of the rectangle. Add two seats below the rim of the boat. Draw in the planking on the outsides of the boat's hull and add some shading inside.

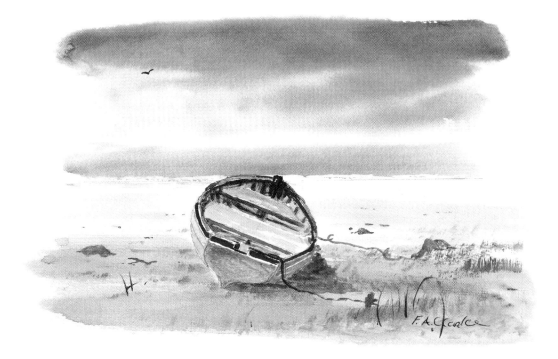

drawing and painting fruit

Drawing fruit is not difficult at all. Each is made up of very basic shapes and if you practise them all individually you'll have no trouble bringing them together in a wonderful still life painting.

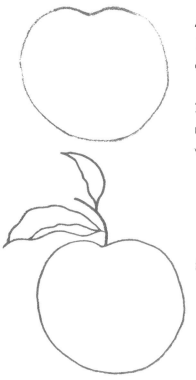

APPLES

1 Draw a circle with a slight dent in the top.

2 Add a stalk. The leaves are really two curved lines that wobble slightly.

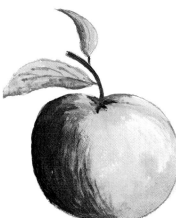

3 With your small brush paint a watery green (90% Lemon yellow with 10% Cobalt blue) onto your apple. Add more blue to darken some patches around its top and bottom and its leaves. Let this dry. With pale Alizarin crimson on your rigger, paint curved strokes on the left side. Add more Alizarin crimson to darken the very left edge. The stalk is Burnt umber, with a little added to your green for the veins and stalk base shadow. Add a white gouache highlight on the right side.

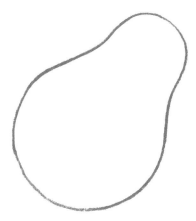

PEARS

1 Draw two ovals.

2 Rub out the lines inside and curve the outside edge to make a pear shape.

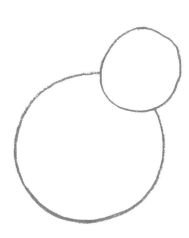

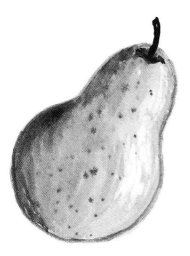

3 With a small brush, paint a pale mix of Lemon yellow and Raw sienna over the pear. With downward curved strokes of a rigger, add Burnt umber patches on the left. While wet, add Burnt umber dots and darken further the very left edge. Use Burnt umber for the stalk and its base. When dry, add white gouache highlights in downward strokes and a tiny dot on the stalk.

Handy tip: When you paint with watercolours, it's useful to know that you always paint from light to dark. You paint the light colours on first so that you can then cover parts of these with the darker colours. It wouldn't work the other way round. As you paint your fruit and build up the paint layers, you'll see what I mean.

BANANAS

1 A banana is just a series of curves. Draw the bottom curve first then draw a parallel curve above it.

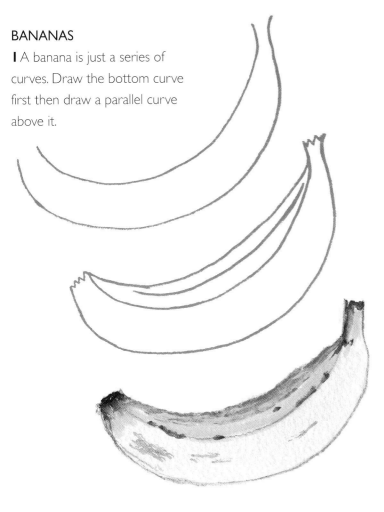

2 Draw two more curves above these, tapering them to meet with the main banana. Add a zigzag line to join up the ends of curves at the end of the banana and another at the stalk end.

3 Use a rigger and paint the whole banana with pale Lemon yellow mixed with a tiny bit of Burnt umber, leaving the odd very small white patch. Add a tiny bit of Cobalt blue and paint the shaded half of the fruit. Add a little more Cobalt blue and slightly darken further the edge of the banana. Use pale Burnt umber to add definition marks following the line curves of the fruit. Use darker Burnt umber for the tail end and stalk top.

CHERRIES

1 Draw three circles not quite in a line.

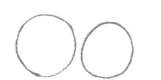

2 Draw the leaves above these – they are just two curved lines meeting at each end and adjusted to have wiggly sides. Draw stalk lines up from the circles to disappear under the leaves and form a bunch.

3 Use a rigger with pale Alizarin crimson to paint the cherries. While wet, mix in more crimson and a bit of Cobalt blue to darken their left sides. The leaves are a Lemon yellow and Cobalt blue mix, adding more blue for the darker, more mottled green patches. Mix Burnt umber with Cobalt blue for the stalks and leaf veins. Add white gouache highlights to each cherry.

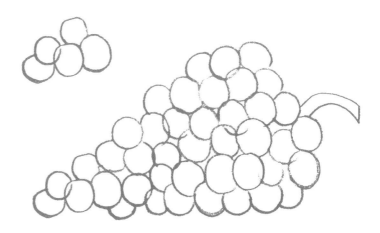

GRAPES

1 Draw one freehand circle.

2 Add other almost-complete circles around your first one.

3 Continue adding to this until you have formed a full bunch of grapes. Remember the bottom of the bunch will be pretty straight as it is lying on a surface. Add a couple of curved lines to form a stalk.

4 With a rigger, paint a mix of Alizarin crimson and Cobalt blue on your grapes. While still wet, add a little more Alizarin crimson, Cobalt blue and some Burnt umber to your mix to darken the left sides of the grapes. When dry, add two dots of white gouache to highlight their right sides. Use Burnt umber for the stalk and then use a dark mix of Alizarin crimson, Cobalt blue and Burnt umber to darken the patches in between the grapes and the underside of the stalk.

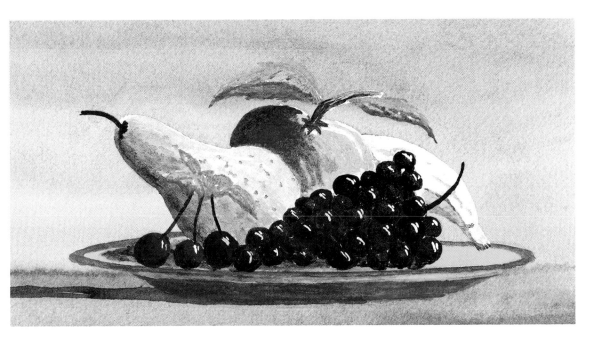

PLATE OF FRUIT

Draw the fruit just above your horizon line. Paint it with masking fluid. Draw the plate under the fruit. When masking fluid is dry, mix some Alizarin crimson, Cobalt blue and Raw sienna with your large brush. Paint in the background from the top of the paper, down to well below the horizon line. While it's still wet, go over the area under the horizon to darken it and give the impression of a tablecloth. Let this dry.

Rub the masking fluid off. Individually paint each fruit: start with those at the top and work down the paper so you don't smudge what you've already painted. (You may want to remask the cherries and grapes while you paint the apple, pear and banana.) When dry, paint the plate a mix of Lemon yellow and Burnt umber and the rim in Cobalt blue. The shadow is Cobalt blue mixed with Alizarin crimson and Raw sienna, and add shadow to the left of the cherries and under the grape bunch, too.

creating flowers with no fuss

Drawing flowers is really not as hard as you might think when you simplify them. They are just a collection of different shapes: if you concentrate on drawing in only the main outlines and ignore the detail, you'll find it much easier. For a vase of flowers, start with one flower and progress. Often we try to paint a huge vase of flowers and get lost, so, keep it simple and start small.

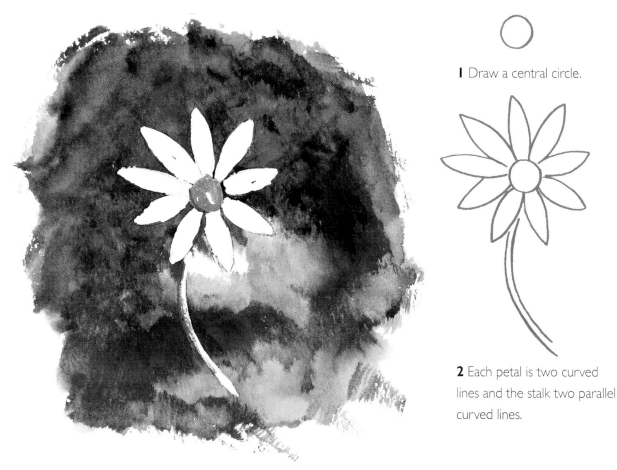

1 Draw a central circle.

2 Each petal is two curved lines and the stalk two parallel curved lines.

3 If you mask your flower with masking fluid, you can then paint in a lovely colourful background. I have used only Lemon yellow, Alizarin crimson and Cobalt blue, mixed with a little water and (cleaning my brush each time) dabbed them onto the paper. When dry, remove the masking fluid and paint in the centre with a mix of Lemon yellow and Alizarin crimson, leaving some tiny patches of white for highlights.

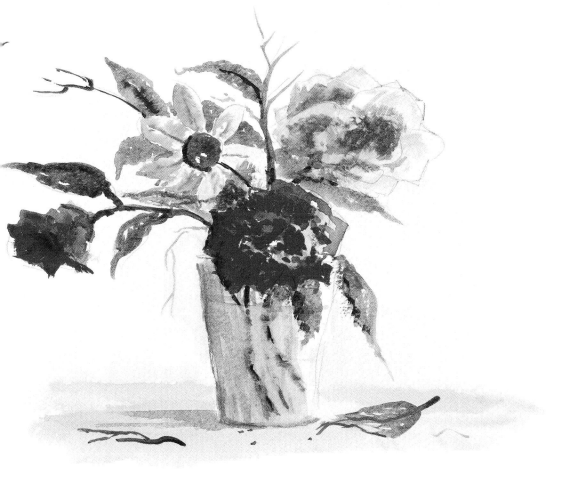

Loosely draw the rough shapes of the flowers and the container. Start in the centre and work out. Paint in a pale background (mix Raw sienna and Cobalt blue) with the small goathair brush. Let this dry. Use Lemon yellow for the top right-hand flower, adding some Alizarin crimson while the paper is still wet. The top left daisy is Lemon yellow mixed with a little Raw sienna, and a mix of Raw sienna and Alizarin crimson for the centre. The two lower flowers are various strengths of Alizarin crimson: start with a watery mix and work up to patches of almost neat paint. With your rigger, mix Lemon yellow and a tiny bit of Cobalt blue for the greener foliage. Paint the glass with a weak mix of Cobalt blue and Raw sienna, going from the left and lightening the paint with more water as you go across. Finish off with Burnt umber mixed with Raw sienna for the stalks.

Handy tip: Always use a clean finger or eraser when removing masking fluid. Rub from the outer edge in towards the middle to avoid the possibility of tearing any painted parts of your paper.

Advice for painting outside

I love painting outdoors, particularly when I'm on holiday. There is nothing in this world to compare with spending a day sitting by the sea or in the mountains, painting. Your picture can be just a rough sketch to use later or a complete painting. All that matters is you do it. But before you embark on your journey let me save you from some of the pitfalls that I have encountered. It's really frustrating to make a trip, only to arrive at the area you would like to paint and discover you have forgotten to bring water, paints or your palette (some of the things I have forgotten more than once). So, I've compiled the checklist below to help you and it now hangs in my studio.

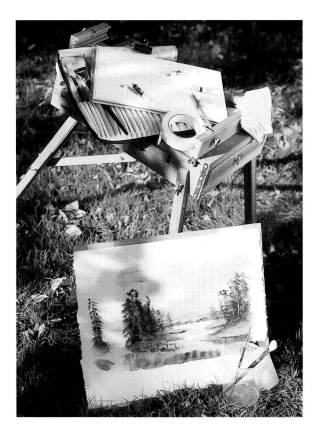

- Brushes: large and small goathair, rigger plus an old brush, if you have one, for masking fluid
- Paints: eight colours plus your white gouache
- Paper
- Palette (I've had to improvise and use the hardboard back of my paper pad more than once!)
- A water container to hold your water (half an old plastic bottle works well)
- Water and cloths
- Pencil, ruler and eraser
- Board and masking tape
- Masking fluid
- Folding stool, if you have one, or something to sit on and lay your materials on as the ground can be damp
- A small, sharp knife (really useful for cutting paper smaller, sharpening your pencil, etc)
- Large plastic bag to protect your paper and, of course, your finished picture

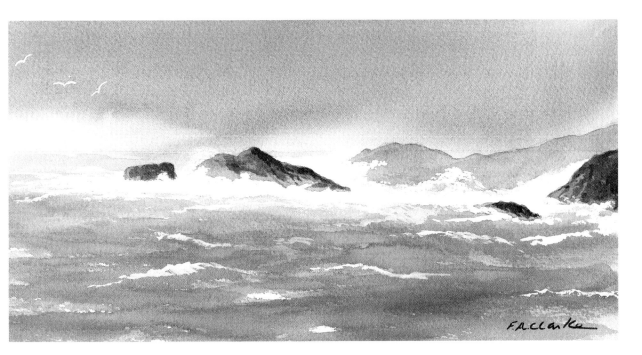

There are a few more things it might be handy to know before you set out. To protect your brush tips when you travel you can take your ruler and, using elastic bands, fix your brushes to it. Make sure the bristles are kept flat against the ruler and that the elastic bands are around the handles only, not squashing the bristles. An easel can be helpful, but it's not vital. My tip on this is to try it out at home first and get used to using it before you head up a rocky mountain with it.

Once you're outdoors, sometimes people find it difficult to paint the whole wide view they see. If you want, you can select just a portion of the landscape to paint by using a viewfinder. You can make an instant one using your thumbs and forefingers to form a square shape. If you then bring your hands up close to your eyes, you can look through your hands to scan along the landscape and select the most pleasing part of the view you'd like to paint. It's handy to take your camera and photograph the view so that if you get rained off you can continue your picture at home later. (See pages 116–17 for some useful advice on painting from a photograph.)

Finally, remember it might rain so bring an umbrella, and don't forget a flask of tea – it always tastes best outdoors for some reason!

Simplifying your photos

I thought it would be helpful to show you how to apply my Have Some More Fun technique to a landscape in a photograph. Often when you look at a view or a picture you want to copy you think you don't know where to start. The horizon, sky, middle and foreground lesson still applies and once you've established these areas you can apply the technique. It helps to sketch out in pencil the position of the main features (see opposite) to compose your painting. Leave out fine detail and look at the overall shapes. Remember you can simplify things, as I have done with the cottage brickwork, windows and stone wall, and you can also add bits – I have extended the out-buildings, put in a fence and added more foreground in front of the wall.

SKY

MIDDLEGROUND
= hills above
horizon line and
the buildings

HORIZON

FOREGROUND
= bushes, grass
and stone wall

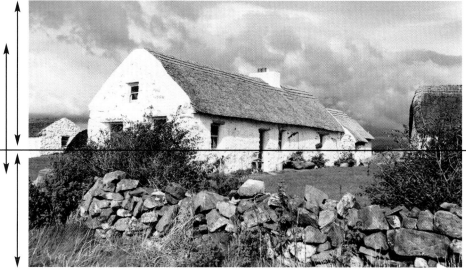

Handy tip: Mixing greens can be tricky, but all you need is a little patience and practise. If you put out your chosen yellow paint first (either Lemon yellow or Raw sienna) and then slowly mix in your blue, a tiny bit at a time, you'll be able to control the mix. There is a never-ending variety of greens you can create so, when you mix one you like, be sure to note it somewhere for future reference.

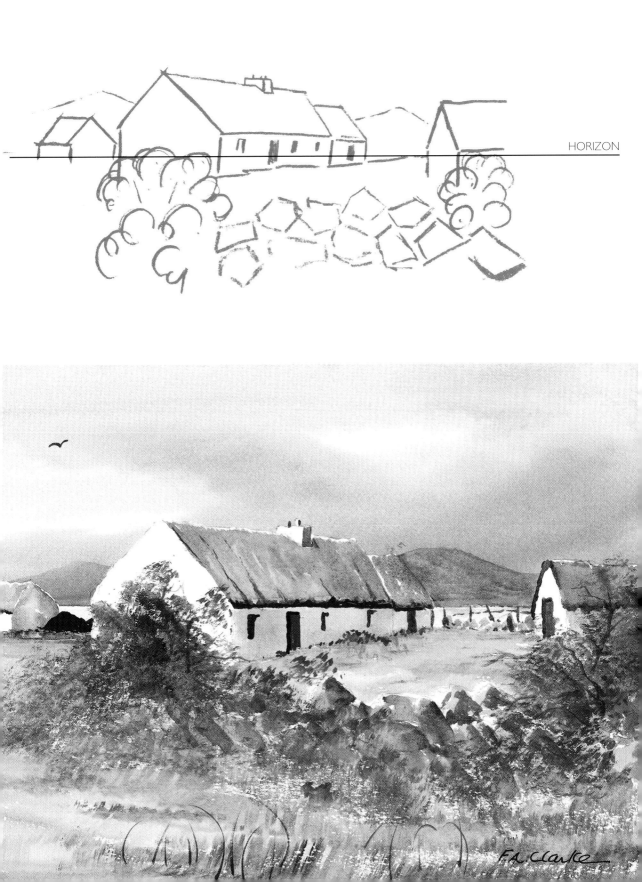

HORIZON

Frequently asked questions

Since I've been teaching people how to paint I've discovered that you all often want to know about the same things. Here are some questions I get asked a lot. I hope the answers help so solve the odd problem you may encounter or just quell your curiosity.

Q: Can I mix different brands of watercolours?

A: Of course you can. Just remember colours may vary, so it's best to stick to one brand if you can for consistency. Stay away from the cheap paints like the ones they sell in discount stores – they contain very little pigment and are often a poor colour representation (see page 14 for further details).

Q: If I start a painting and have to interrupt my session, can I go back to it later?

A: Yes. It's a good idea not to wash your paints off your palette though. You can easily revive the paint with a little water if it dries out, but it will be hard to get exactly the same colour mix again to match your already painted bits.

Q: What do I do if I haven't made enough of a paint mixture, when mixing two colours? I don't seem to ever be able to match the colour.

A: This is where keeping a record of colour mixes is so useful. When you're painting, add to your colour wheel (see pages 120-1) so you can refer back and refresh your memory on what colours you've made and how you've made them. Mixing and testing colours does take time, but noting them down becomes second nature after a while.

Q: When I put on my masking fluid to keep some areas white, I forgot to cover some of the things I should have covered. Now I've mistakenly painted over that area and it is coloured instead of white. What can I do?

A: First wet the part of your picture that you want to whiten. Dab it with a tissue to help remove most of the colour. This may not remove all the pigment, but don't worry. Dry the picture then use your White gouache to paint the area you want to whiten. It may take two coats but it will work.

Q: If I make a big mistake and want to change a large part of my picture can I clean it off? I have been told it is not possible to alter watercolours.

A: It is possible to alter your painting, but do be careful. If the error is large and covers a big area of the paper (across to an edge), you can actually hold that part of the painting under slowly running cold water. Use a clean, small flat brush and gently rub at the wetted paint you want to remove. Brush the watered-off paint away from the rest of the painting and off the edge of the paper. It will take a little time and patience but it is possible. When the paper is dry you can repaint that section of your picture. For smaller mistakes you'll often find that a little clean water on a brush applied to the mistake, then blotted off with a clean tissue, can help remove enough of the paint for you to be able to clear the decks and paint over that patch when dry. Repeat the wetting, blotting process if necessary but don't scrub hard at the paper or it will disintegrate.

Q: When I purchased my rigger brush it had a small plastic tube protecting the bristles. Should I replace it after use?

A: Mmmm! I don't because it's very difficult not to catch a few of the bristles and bend them. I have seen people trying to replace these tubes and think it is like trying to thread a rope through the eye of a needle. However, they are one way of keeping bristles straight when you're travelling, so, if you are really confident, have great eyesight and lots of patience you might want to store your rigger in its tube. But be extremely careful.

Q: I have been told it is not right to copy, that it's cheating and not real 'art'. What do you think?

A: This always makes me mad when I hear so-called experts saying this. Of course it's all right for you to copy from other things. Painting any view is making a copy of it, and so is painting a portrait making a copy of a face. If you look back through history you'll see that many of the great artists have painted the same views or people. In fact, if you visit any public art gallery you'll find students making copies of the great artworks found there – not to sell, but to learn how the great artists created these works.

Q: What are warm and cool colours?

A: If you imagine cold, the colour blue comes to mind, and if you think warm, red comes to mind. Warm and cool colours are exactly this, with warm colours being the reds, oranges and yellows and cool colours being the blues and purples.

Colour mixing

As with my last book, I have kept the colour mixing section until the end. I really do believe that we must paint pictures first, before we get bogged down with the complications of colour mixing. Colour charts or colour wheels can be useful to teach us about mixing colours, but only once you've been encouraged by your efforts and proved to yourself that you can paint a picture. By now I hope you've done that.

MAKING A COLOUR WHEEL

There are three primary colours: red, blue and yellow. By mixing any combination of these three colours we can, in theory, produce every other colour which exists. Making a colour wheel shows us what colour we get when we mix two colours together, and having one provides you with an instant reminder if ever you are puzzled about how you originally created a particular colour. It saves time if you're trying to recreate a colour, as a glance at your record will tell you how to mix it up again.

I am sure you have realized, as you have been painting, that it takes more time to mix the right colour than it does to actually apply it to your picture. I always maintain it takes about 90% of your time to mix your paint and only about 10% to put it on your paper. So you can see the advantage of having a colour wheel of your own, to help and guide you.

Don't spend ages making a colour wheel – a quick one like this, using our eight colours, will help you understand how colour mixing works. All you do is paint a patch of each colour, as they are from the tube, in a circle or down the side of your paper if you prefer. Then, in turn, mix each with the one next to it (e.g. Ultramarine blue with Light red) in equal amounts and paint the resulting colour in a block between them. Now when you refer to your wheel you will easily see the colour you'll get if you mix these two colours together. Clean your brush and continue mixing one colour with the next on the wheel until you have eight new colour mixes.

There are of course hundreds of colours you can make from your original eight. It depends on which two you add to each other (and whether you add a third colour, too), and what proportion of each you mix. And remember, a shade of any colour mixed can always be lightened by adding more water.

When you're painting pictures and find a colour you like, add it to your wheel and note the paint mix. It really will save you time when you next want to use it. Every artist does this so you should because, yes, you are an artist!

Gallery

My gallery is to provide you with lots of extra paintings to try. I've noted the paint colours you'll need and added the occasional tip where necessary, but now you're more confident and practised you should be able to think out how to paint them for yourselves. Don't forget the golden rule: Horizon, Sky, Middle and Foreground. Go on, surprise yourself . . . HAVE SOME MORE FUN!

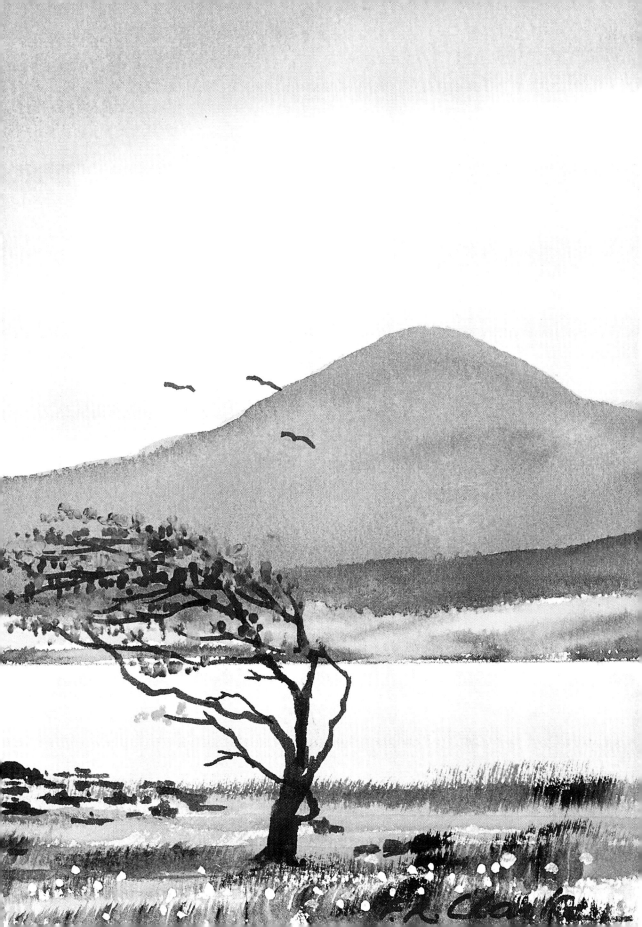

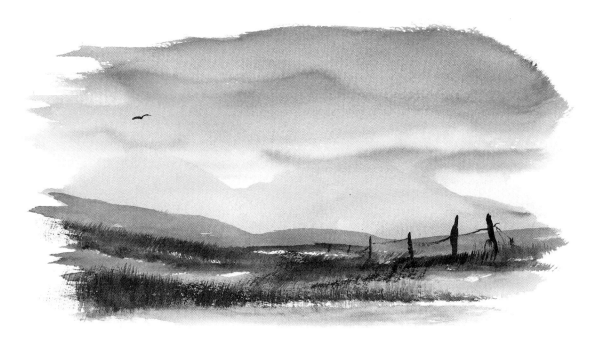

Use Lemon yellow, Alizarin crimson, Ultramarine blue and Burnt umber. This painting really shows how you can use a limited number of colours to great effect.

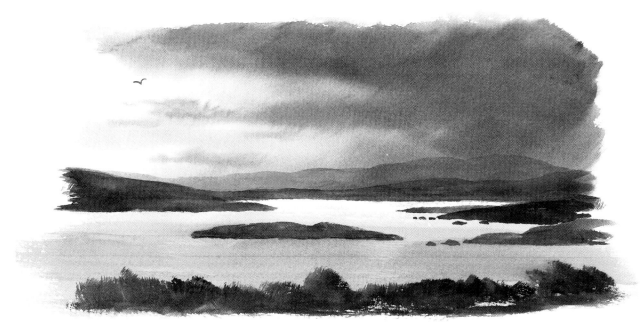

Use Raw sienna, Alizarin crimson and Payne's grey for the sky; Raw sienna and Alizarin crimson for the water; Payne's grey and Alizarin crimson for the rocks; and White gouache for the light on the water.

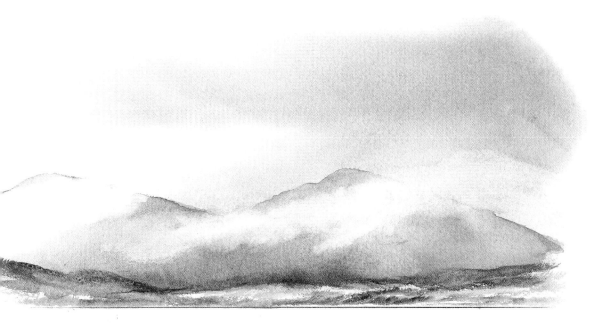

Use Cobalt blue and Light red for the sky and mountains. Dab out paint, while still wet, with a clean tissue to form the mist. The foreground is Lemon yellow, Cobalt blue and Raw sienna.

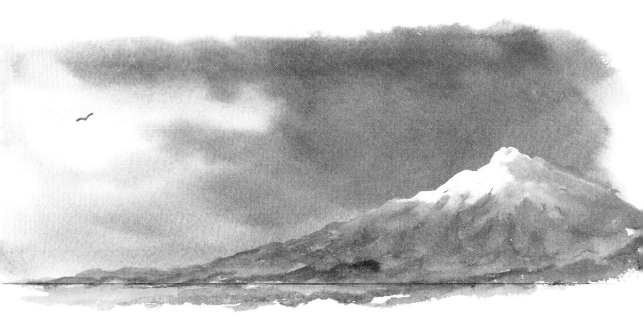

Wet the sky area and paint it using Raw sienna, then Ultramarine blue, then add Alizarin crimson and Raw sienna to the blue. The mountain is different mixes of these same colours, with White gouache for the peak.

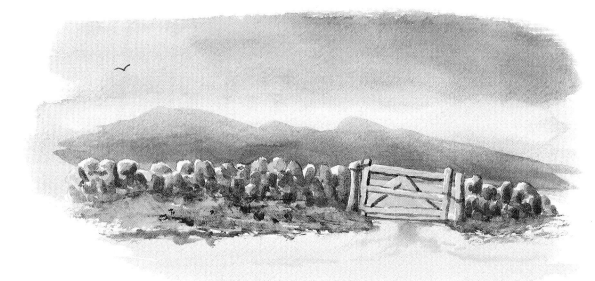

Mask the gate and wall. The sky and mountains are Ultramarine blue and Light red. Use a Lemon yellow and Raw sienna wash for middleground, remove the masking fluid and use light and dark mixes of Raw sienna and Ultramarine blue for the wall stones and road. The grass is Lemon yellow with Ultramarine blue.

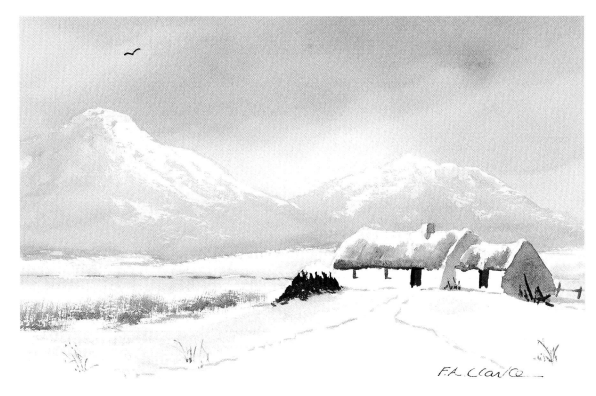

Use Raw sienna, then Alizarin crimson and Cobalt blue for the sky and the same for the mountains, lake and shaded foreground. The cottage roof is Raw sienna and Burnt umber and the turf pile is Burnt umber. Use White gouache to create snow on the mountains, roof and turf pile.

RIGHT Draw a rectangle with triangles on each end for the boat hull, straight lines for the mast and booms, and triangles for the sails. Use Ultramarine blue, Light red and Burnt umber.

BELOW The sky's Cobalt blue and Light red, then add Raw sienna to these for the mountains. The sea's Cobalt blue and Lemon yellow. Sand and rocks are Raw sienna and Burnt umber, and the seagulls White gouache and Burnt umber.

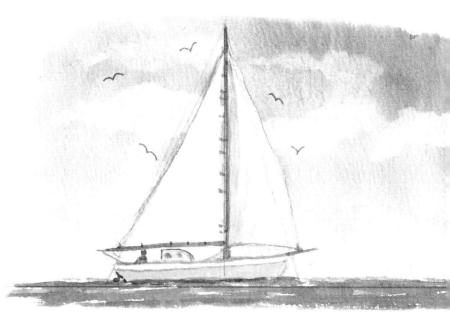

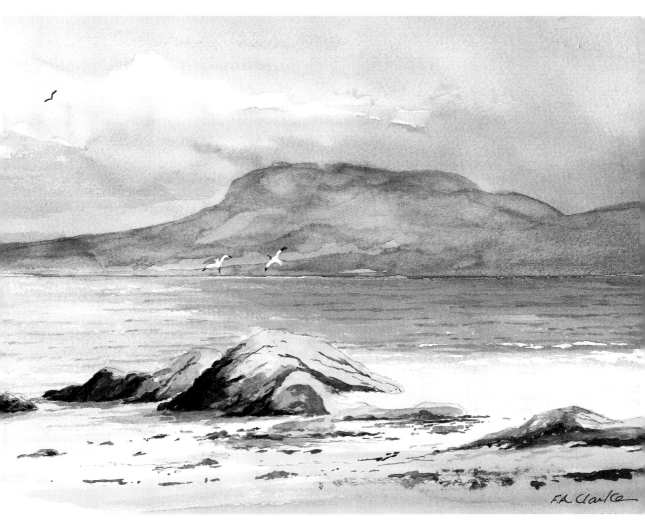

And finally . . .

Well, that's all for this book. I hope you have enjoyed *Paintbox 2*, painted lots of beautiful pictures and proved my theory that anyone can paint. I really hope I've made watercolour painting as simple as possible and you've achieved great things, as well as having had fun.

I feel it's important to give you the full lists of materials you need and instructions (starting at the very beginning) on how to use them, and just as you can make up a recipe from a good cookery book you should be able to create a wonderful painting with the right ingredients and instructions. It may seem very unartistic to some people to go about painting in this way, comparing painting to cooking, but I feel absolutely sure there is a real similarity. It's funny, we often talk about 'the art of cookery' and both painting and cookery *are* art. They are creative, therapeutic and bring much pleasure to those who partake. I am sure you now have plenty of material to encourage the creative side of your brain and get the benefits that using it will bring you.

One of the many mistaken beliefs about learning to paint is that we will all end up painting like our teachers. This could not be further from the truth, and to quote a very famous art teacher, Robert Henri, 'No matter how hard you try, your own style will shine through.' So don't worry, we won't all be producing exactly the same paintings and you won't all be painting like me!

If you have difficulty obtaining any of the materials we use in this book, please contact me at:

Frank Clarke
P O Box 3312
Dublin 6W
Ireland
Freephone: 0800 0182541(UK) or 01850 510810 (Ireland)

Or visit my website: www.simplypainting.com